Stan Lee PRESENTS THE MIGHTY MARVEL® SUPERHEROES' COOKBOOK

OUR RECIPES TASTE AND SMELL MARVEL-OUS!

Created by Gene Malis
Recipes by Jody Cameron Malis
  of Celebrity Kitchen, Inc.
Art by Joe Giella

A Fireside Book Published by Simon and Schuster, New York

Published by Simon and Schuster
A Division of Gulf & Western Corporation
Simon & Schuster Building
Rockefeller Center
1230 Avenue of the Americas
New York, New York 10020

Manufactured in the United States of America
1   2   3   4   5   6   7   8   9   10

Library of Congress Cataloging in Publication Data
Main entry under title:
Stan Lee Presents THE MIGHTY MARVEL SUPERHEROES' COOKBOOK.
(A Fireside book)
SUMMARY: Easy recipes for a variety of snacks,
main dishes, desserts, and beverages illustrated with characters
from Mighty Marvel comics.
Includes index.
1. Cookery — Juvenile literature. [1. Cookery] I. Lee, Stan.
II. Malis, Gene. III. Malis, Jody Cameron. IV. Presnick, Stan.
V. Title: the mighty marvel superheroes' cookbook.
TX652.5.S63   641.5   77-2858
ISBN 0-671-22559-6

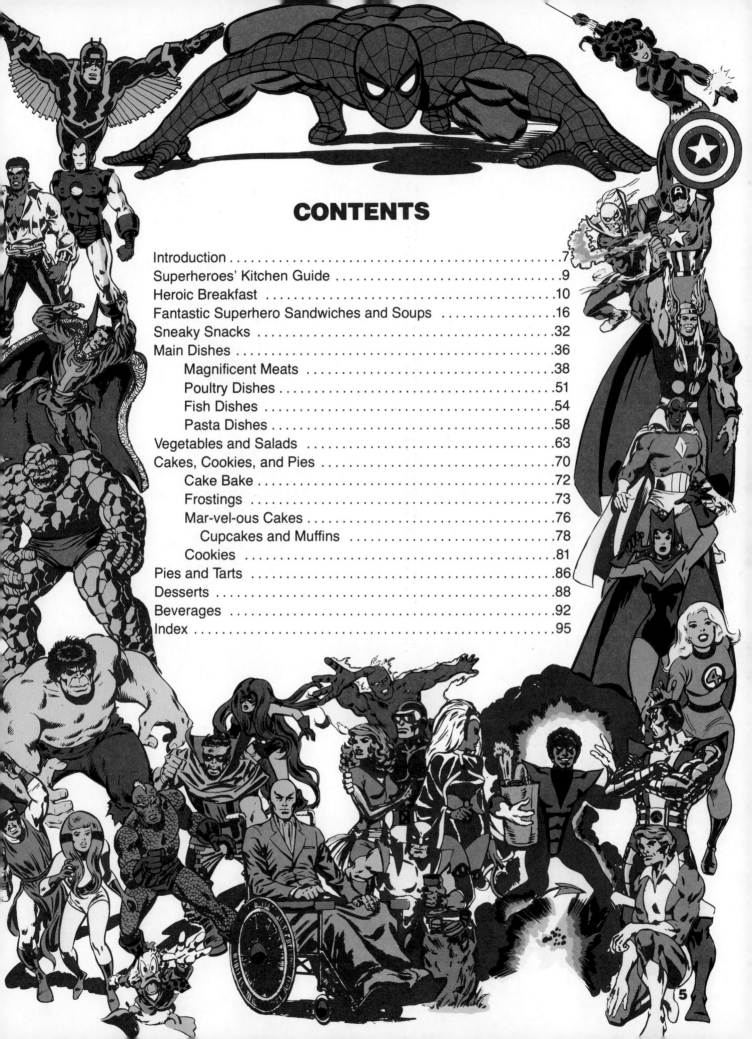

CONTENTS

Introduction

Do Superheroes ever find the time to eat? You bet they do! Awhile back some young fan asked us this question and it got us to thinking that perhaps many other fans might be interested in just what our Superheroes like to eat. After all, good meals are mighty important when one leads the exciting, active lives that they do!

After doing a bit of research we were thrilled to discover that Superhero recipes were super sensational! Then, we asked ourselves, why not let the whole wide world in on these novel, delicious dishes! And the result of this thought is right here in your hands, dear reader — the world's first (and only) Superhero cookbook!!! Now, you and your palate can enjoy another great adventure with your favorite Superheroes!

SUPERHEROES' KITCHEN GUIDE

Do's and Don'ts!!

- Turn the handle of a pan inward or toward the back of the range to prevent the pan from being knocked off the range.

- When removing the lid from a pan, tilt the top of the lid away from you so that the steam will rise away from you.

- Don't reach over an open flame.

- Don't stand too close to the range. Remember that hair and clothing can catch fire easily.

- Don't fill a saucepan so full that it can boil over and put out the flame. If this should happen, turn off the heat and open the window.

- When you use a vegetable parer, always point the blade away from you.

Be Neat!!

DON'T FORGET TO CLEAN UP THE MESS IN THE KITCHEN! IT'S EASIER TO CLEAN AS YOU GO ALONG THAN TO LEAVE IT FOR LATER.

Safety First!!

- Always strike a match away from you.

- To avoid burns, use pot holders to pick up hot utensils.

- When you use a knife, keep your fingers out of the way and cut away from you.

- If grease in a pan or a broiler catches fire, turn the heat off at once. Then smother fire with flour or salt, never water.

- When you pour hot liquids from a saucepan, hold the lid in place to prevent the food from spilling out. Stand in such a way that the steam will not burn your face. If the contents of a pan are too heavy, place a colander in the sink and pour liquid and food into it. Then put the food back into the pan.

Nothing will start your day better than a nourishing breakfast. It will give you the stamina to work through the morning without getting that let-down feeling before lunch. After all, it's been a long time since you fed your body cells. All Superheroes know that the body, like any well-running machine, needs a constant supply of fuel to continue performing at its best. So let's start the day right with Captain America's DAY STARTERS!

VIP AND VINEGAR!

CAPTAIN AMERICA
DAY STARTERS!

**fruit juice
pancakes
milk**

A fresh fruit or fruit juice. Lots of vitamins C and A. Good for healthy gums and body tissues, growth, and healthy skin.

**cereal with fruit
milk**

Milk is the best source of calcium. It's needed for strong bones and teeth. It also supplies protein — essential building blocks for our bodies. Eggs or cheese are also good breakfast starters!

**fruit juice   toast
eggs   milk
bacon**

Bread or cereal ... lots of variations in this department. These foods supply the carbohydrates that give heat and energy. Make up your own menus and start your day right!

HULK'S FRIED POTATOES

WITH BACON AND EGGS

To cook the type of eggs you choose, turn to page 12.

To cook bacon: Place bacon strips in large frying pan. Heat over medium flame. When one side is done, use tongs or fork to turn bacon to second side. When done and crisp looking, place bacon strips on paper towel to drain.

Serves 4

    1 cup cooking oil
    2 cups frozen potato strips, or 4 medium
      potatoes, pared and cut into strips
    1 onion, thinly sliced
    ½ teaspoon garlic salt
    ¼ teaspoon pepper

In large frying pan, heat oil over medium flame. Carefully slide potato strips into oil. Add onion slices, garlic salt, and pepper. Cook until potatoes are lightly browned, about 15 minutes, turning often. When done, remove to paper towel and drain.

EGGS AND SUCH

Hard-Boiled Eggs

Place eggs in saucepan and add enough cold water to cover the eggs. Turn heat to medium high and cook eggs until water starts to bubble. Reduce heat to low and cook eggs for ten minutes. Remove pan from heat and let stand for five minutes. When time is up, immediately run cold water over eggs. Remove eggshells by cracking the surface and peeling carefully.

Soft-Boiled Eggs

Cook eggs in the same way that you cooked the Hard-Boiled Eggs except limit the time to five minutes instead of ten. Remove pan from heat and let stand for two minutes. Lift egg with tablespoon and run cold water on it. Scoop out egg from shell with a teaspoon.

Scrambled Eggs

Break eggs into bowl. Beat with fork. Melt butter or margarine in frying pan over medium heat. Tilt pan so that pan is coated. Lower the heat. Pour in eggs. Cook slowly, turning eggs with spatula as eggs start to set at the bottom of pan. Eggs should be moist and shiny looking. Turn off heat and serve eggs on plate. Add salt and pepper.

Fried Eggs

Melt margarine or butter in frying pan over medium-high heat. Lower heat. One at a time, break eggs into a cup, and gently glide them into frying pan. Cover and cook for two or three minutes. Remove eggs with pancake turner.

Baked Eggs

Turn oven temperature to 350 degrees F. Grease pie plate with butter. One at a time, break eggs into cup and pour into pie plate, being careful not to crowd or overlap. Sprinkle with salt and pepper. Bake in oven for 15 minutes.

Deviled Eggs

Make Hard-Boiled Eggs as instructed above. Cut eggs into halves carefully; gently remove yolks and put into bowl. Mash yolks with fork; add mayonnaise and mustard and mix lightly. Pile egg yolk mixture into the whites. Sprinkle paprika over top and chill.

Variations:
Prepare recipe for Deviled Eggs, adding 2 tablespoons of deviled ham spread or peanut butter or pickle relish to yolk mixture.

Pancakes

If you are using a mix, follow the manufacturer's instructions on the box for mixing, THEN:
Lightly grease frying pan with 1 tablespoon of shortening. Heat pan over medium heat until shortening is melted and pan is coated. Pour a little of the batter into the pan. It will spread to form a round patty. When the top of the pancake is covered with bubbles and the edges look dry, turn the pancake with a pancake turner to brown the other side.

Pancake Variations:

Jelly Roll Pancakes   When pancakes are done, spread your favorite jelly over the top. Roll up each pancake and put a toothpick in the center to hold it in place.

Applesauce Pancakes   When making the batter, add ½ cup of applesauce and mix together with other ingredients.

Cheese Pancakes   Cut 1 slice of American cheese into tiny strips. Add the cheese strips to the pancake batter and mix.

Peanut Butter Pancakes   When making batter, add 3 tablespoons of creamy peanut butter and mix with other ingredients.

Ice Cream Pancakes   Cook pancakes as directed. When done, place a scoop of vanilla ice cream on top and pour your favorite topping over all.

French Toast   Makes 4 slices

Break 2 eggs into bowl. Add ½ cup milk and beat with egg beater. Grease frying pan. Dip bread into egg mixture and soak well. Place bread slices in frying pan and brown each side over medium heat. Use a pancake turner to remove from pan to serving plate. Sprinkle with syrup, cinnamon, wheat germ, or brown sugar.

THE THING'S CLOBBERED OMELET

Serves 4

- ¼ cup chopped pepper
- ¼ cup chopped onion
- ¼ cup butter or margarine
- 1 can (8½ ounces) mixed vegetables, drained
- 1 can (10½ ounces) condensed cream of mushroom soup
- 8 eggs, slightly beaten

Cook pepper and onion in butter or margarine until tender. Add mixed vegetables. Blend in soup and eggs. Cook over low heat until eggs are set, lifting eggs gently now and then. When done, divide into 4 equal portions and serve hot with chili sauce or catsup.

HOW SWEET IT IS!!

SPIDEY'S CHOCOLATE WEB PANCAKES

Prepare pancakes according to the instructions on the package. When done, stack on serving plate and form a web by criss crossing lines with liquid chocolate syrup across the top.

WASP'S BREAKFAST FRUIT BOWL

Serves 4

I'LL KEEP THE FLIES AWAY!

1 can (8½ ounces) pear halves
1 can (8½ ounces) fruit cocktail
2 medium-sized bananas, peeled
   and cut into thin slices
1 can (8½ ounces) peach slices

In each of four serving bowls, alternate and divide evenly, pear halves, scoops of fruit cocktail, and banana slices; top with peach slices.

Variations: Select other favorite fruits for the Breakfast Fruit Bowl, such as melon balls, mandarin oranges, grapes, strawberries, grapefruit sections, and pineapple. Instead of a bowl, you can use a cantaloupe as a base by cutting it in half and removing the seeds. Then place your selection of fruits inside the cavity and enjoy.

HAWKEYE'S

CORNED BEEF HASH

Serves 4

1 teaspoon salad oil
   or shortening
1 can (16½ ounces) corned beef hash
1 can (8½ ounces) Mexican-style
   kernel corn, drained
2 tablespoons catsup

Heat salad oil or shortening in frying pan over low heat. Add corned beef hash and mash with fork; stir. Add corn and catsup and stir. Cook for 5 minutes, stirring often. Serve hot over toast.

Variations: Hawkeye's Corned Beef Hash can be served with scrambled or fried eggs or as a topping for an open sandwich.
   How many more ways can you think of to serve this delicious recipe?

GALACTUS'

"HE-MAN" PANCAKES

Make pancakes larger in size than usual. When done, place on plate. Fill with any of the following selections by placing the mixture along the center of pancake. Then roll it up and secure it with toothpicks. It's more convenient to use a fork and knife when eating this tasty pancake than to pick it up. Swiss cheese and jelly; applesauce topped with cinnamon; hot cooked cereal with honey and raisins; Sloppy Joe mixture; meat spreads; sliced franks and beans.

TRY THESE!

WHET YOUR APPETITE!

SUB-MARINER'S SUBMARINE

Serves 2

1 can (7 ounces) tuna, drained and flaked
⅓ cup chopped celery
¼ cup mayonnaise
4 bread slices
12 cooked baby shrimp
lettuce leaves

In bowl, combine tuna, celery, and mayonnaise and mix well. Spread bread slices with mayonnaise. Spread tuna mixture on 2 bread slices. Arrange baby shrimp on top of tuna. Top with lettuce and remaining bread.

TORCH'S FIREBALL

Serves 4

¼ cup chopped onion
1 tablespoon margarine
½ pound ground beef
½ cup cooked rice
½ teaspoon dry mustard
½ teaspoon chili powder
2 cans (8 ounces each) tomato sauce
¾ cup water
4 hamburger buns, split and toasted

Sauté onions in margarine in large frying pan until lightly browned. Add beef and brown evenly. Add rice, mustard, chili powder, tomato sauce, and water. Cook over low heat for 10 minutes, stirring often. Spoon about 1/2 cup of mixture on each bun half and close; or you may divide equal portions of mixture onto each bun half and serve as an open sandwich.

HULK'S SLOPPY JOE

UMMMM...

Serves 2

1 can (16 ounces) Sloppy Joe mixture
4 frankfurter rolls
 mustard

Pour Sloppy Joe mixture into saucepan. Heat over low heat for 5 minutes or until hot. Spread mustard on rolls. Then spread hot Sloppy Joe mixture onto rolls. Close rolls and enjoy.

GOOEY CHEESE!

SPIDEY'S PARMIGIANI

Serves 4

¼ cup mayonnaise
2 teaspoons prepared mustard
8 slices white bread
8 slices Mozzarella cheese

4 thin slices cooked ham
2 eggs
¾ cup milk
3 tablespoons margarine

In bowl, combine mayonnaise and mustard; mix well. Lay out bread slices. Spread mixture on each slice. Alternate cheese slices and ham slices on 4 bread slices. Top with remaining bread slices. In pie plate, beat eggs and milk together. Dip sandwiches into egg mixture and coat both sides well. Heat margarine in frying pan over medium heat. Brown sandwiches on both sides until nicely browned.

CAPTAIN AMERICA'S AMERICANA HERO

Serves 6

½ cup (1 stick) margarine
¼ cup prepared mustard
2 loaves French bread

6 slices boiled ham
6 slices Swiss cheese

Cream margarine and mustard together until well blended. Slice bread in half lengthwise. Spread with margarine-mustard mixture. Arrange ham and cheese on split loaves. Replace tops. Wrap loaves individually in foil, sealing both ends tightly. Bake in hot oven (450 degrees F) for 15 minutes. When done, cut loaves into serving pieces and serve hot.

4 HULKBURGER

KUNG FU BURGER

TORCH'S CHARBURGER

THOR'S THUNDERBURG

1
Kung Fu Burger
Serves 4

- 1 pound ground beef
- 2 tablespoons soy sauce
- 1 can (16½ ounces) Chinese chow mein
- 1 can (16½ ounces) dry Chinese noodles
- 4 hamburger buns

In bowl, combine meat, soy sauce, and Chinese chow mein; mix well. Place in baking dish and bake in oven at 350 degrees F for 25 minutes. When done, place on buns and serve with Chinese noodles.

for more
delicious recipes
turn the page

2

Torch's Char Burger

Serves 4

1 pound ground beef
3 tablespoons chopped onion
1 teaspoon salt
½ teaspoon garlic salt

2 frankfurters, sliced into penny slices
  barbecue sauce
4 frankfurter buns

In bowl, combine all ingredients except sauce and buns; mix well. Shape into four small loaves. Flatten them a little with spatula. Brush with sauce. Broil in oven 5 inches from heat for about 10 minutes. Use pancake turner to turn loaves; brush with sauce. Cook second side 10 minutes. When done, place loaves on buns.

3

Thor's Thunderburg

Serves 4

1 pound ground beef
1 can (8½ ounces) kernel corn
1 teaspoon salt

2 tablespoons pickle relish
1 tablespoon prepared mustard
4 buns

In bowl, combine all ingredients except buns; mix well. Shape into 4 patties. Place in large frying pan and cook over medium heat 10 minutes. Turn and cook second side about 8 minutes. When done, serve on buns.

4

The Hulkburger

Serves 4

1 pound ground beef
1 teaspoon onion salt
1 teaspoon salt
2 tablespoons catsup
2 tablespoons milk

6 buns, split in half
2 medium sized tomatoes,
  thinly sliced
  lettuce leaves

In bowl, combine first five ingredients, and mix well. Form into 8 patties. Place in baking pan and bake in oven at 350 degrees F for 25 minutes. When done, lay out buns. On four bun halves, stack tomato slice, hamburger patty, lettuce, bun half, second hamburger patty, second tomato slice. Close sandwich with third bun half.

HEROIC COMBOS

The Great Triple-Decker Sandwich   Serves 1

- 3 slices bread, toasted
  margarine or butter
- 2 slices bologna
  catsup
  lettuce leaf
- 1 slice of your favorite cheese
- 1 slice tomato
- 4 Spanish olives

Lay bread flat, and spread margarine or butter on each slice. Place bologna slices on one bread slice. Top with a little catsup. Place second bread slice on top of bologna. Place lettuce leaf, cheese and tomato slices on top of second bread slice. Place third bread slice on top. Gently press bread together. Cut into quarters. Stick in toothpicks to hold sandwiches together. Stick an olive on each toothpick.

Hot Open-Faced Sandwiches

Place 2 slices of bread on a plate, side by side. Place slices of either canned or leftover cooked turkey, chicken, roast beef, ham, or other favorites on each slice of bread. Pour ½ cup hot gravy over meat and bread. An open sandwich can be a whole meal. Just serve with potatoes or noodles and a vegetable.
Canned or powdered instant gravies are tasty and convenient to use. Follow the label directions for the amount you need.

Grilled Cheese Sandwich   Serves 2

- 4 slices bread
- 4 slices American processed cheese
- 2 tablespoons margarine

Place 2 cheese slices between two bread slices. Melt margarine in frying pan over low heat. Tilt pan to cover. Place sandwiches in pan and heat one side until browned. Then turn to brown other side.

Variations: Add 2 tomato slices for Grilled Cheese and Tomato sandwich.

Add 2 cooked bacon slices for Grilled Cheese with Bacon.

Add 1 ham slice for Grilled Cheese with Ham.

You can make up many more by following the basic recipe.

Stuffed Franks   Serves 4

- 4 frankfurters
- ¼ cup coarsely grated Cheddar cheese
- 2 tablespoons creamy peanut butter
- 4 partially cooked slices bacon

In bowl, mix cheese and peanut butter. Split frankfurters lengthwise, but not all the way through. Stuff frankfurters with mixture; wrap each one with a bacon slice. Fasten ends with toothpicks. Arrange frankfurters on broiler rack, about 6 inches from heat. Broil 5 minutes.

Cold Open-Faced Sandwiches
The Salabean   Serves 2

- prepared mustard
- 2 slices bread
- 2 slices salami
- 4 tablespoons baked beans

Spread mustard on bread slices. Place salami on top of each slice. Top with 2 tablespoons of baked beans in the center of each slice.

The Liver-Swiss   Serves 2

- 2 tablespoons mayonnaise
- 2 slices bread
- 4 tablespoons liverwurst spread or
- 2 slices of liverwurst
- 2 slices Swiss cheese
- 2 tomato slices

Spread mayonnaise on bread slices; spread on liverwurst or place liverwurst slices on top. Add Swiss cheese and tomato. Serve with potato chips and pickle.

You can use any combinations of sandwich foods to make open-faced sandwiches. Try using different types of bread; one slice can be whole wheat and the other, a slice of rye bread. One slice can be toasted, the other not. Get the idea?

JOLLY SANDWICH MAKER!

MR. FANTASTIC'S BIG JAW BREAKER!

Spread mustard or mayonnaise on 3 bread slices.

Place lettuce leaf and ham on first bread slice. Place second bread slice on top. Place cheese and tomato slices on top.

Place third slice of bread on top. Gently press sandwich together. Cut in half. Top with pickle slice.

PANTHER'S SNACK

WITH CHIPS

Trim the crust from the ends of the bread slices. Spread bread slices with your favorite filling. Cut sandwiches in fourths to make tiny squares.

Soups are popular and good tasting anytime. They can be served before dinner or as a main dish, served hot or cold or as a pick-me-up. Plain soups become great soups when you add such decorative finishing touches as minced parsley, minced chives, grated cheese, thin lemon slices, thin celery rings or croutons.

Lima Bean Chowder

Serves 2

    1 (10 ounce) package frozen lima beans in cheese sauce
    1 small onion, minced
    2 tablespoons margarine
    2 cups milk
    salt and pepper
    croutons

Defrost lima beans by boiling in saucepan for 6 minutes. Fry onion in margarine until transparent. Stir in lima beans, milk, salt and pepper and heat slowly. Stir. Pour into serving bowls and top with croutons.

THOR'S

ASGARDIAN VEGETABLE SOUP

Serves 4

- ½ pound ground beef
- ¼ cup chopped onion
- 1 can (16 ounces) mixed vegetables, drained (save liquid)
- 1 can (10¾) ounces condensed vegetable soup
  liquid from mixed vegetables

In large saucepan, brown beef and onion over low heat for about 10 minutes. Stir in remaining ingredients. Heat 10 minutes, stirring often. Serve hot.

PEAS!

IRON MAN'S
Splendid Split Pea Soup   Serves 4

- 1 can (11 ounces) condensed split pea soup
- 1 soup can water
- 1 can (8 ounces) baby lima beans
- 1 cup croutons

In large saucepan, combine soup and water. Use an egg beater to mix into a smooth mixture. Add lima beans. Heat over low flame about 10 minutes, stirring often. Serve hot and top with croutons.

SILVER SURFER'S SURFBOARD SENSATION

Serves 4

- 1 can (10¾ ounces) condensed mushroom soup
- 1 can (10¾ ounces) condensed tomato soup
- 1 teaspoon curry powder
- 2 cups light cream
- 1 cup baby shrimp

Combine soups, curry powder and cream in the top of 'a double-boiler pan. Place over gently boiling water and heat well. Stir occasionally to blend thoroughly. Add shrimp. Continue cooking until shrimp is heated.

Soup Is Good Tasting Anytime!

Franks and Vegetable Soup

Serves 2

- 2 frankfurters, sliced in penny slices
- 1 tablespoon margarine
- 1 envelope dried vegetable soup mix

Brown frank slices in margarine. Add vegetable soup mix and the amount of water specified on the label. Heat 15 minutes over low heat. Serve hot with crackers.

Meatball Soup

Serves 2

- 1 can (10½ ounces) condensed tomato soup
- ½ soup can water
- 1 can (16 ounces) meatballs

Empty soup can into saucepan and stir. Add water, a little at a time and stir. Heat over medium-high flame and boil 3 minutes. Lower heat and add meatballs. Cook 3 minutes more. Serve hot.

Fishy Vegetable Soup

Serves 2

- 1 can (10¾ ounces) condensed cream of mushroom soup
- ½ soup can water
- 1 can (3½ ounces) chunk tuna, drained and flaked

Pour vegetable soup into saucepan. Add water and stir. Add tuna and stir again. Cover and cook over medium heat for 5 minutes or until hot. Remove lid and stir soup while cooking 3 minutes more. Serve over rice or toast, or as is.

Meaty Soup

Serves 2

- ½ cup cooked meat, cut in strips
- 1 tablespoon margarine
- 1 can (10½ ounces) condensed tomato soup
- 1 soup can milk
- 1 can (16 ounces) mixed vegetables, drained

Cook meat in margarine until lightly browned. Add remaining ingredients. Heat through, stirring often. Serve hot with crackers or toast.

Cheese Soup

Serves 4

- 1 can (10½ ounces) Cheddar cheese soup
- 1 soup can water
- ½ cup croutons, or bread crumbs, or pretzels, or potato chips

Pour soup and water into saucepan and stir. Cook over low heat for 5 minutes. Do not boil. Turn off heat. Use ladle to pour soup into serving bowls. Sprinkle croutons, bread crumbs, pretzels, or potato chips on top and stir.

COLD KABOBS

Cold kabobs are great! They are easy to make and the combinations are endless. Skewers, fondue spears, or potato-baking nails can be used. Just make sure they are clean.

Spearhead ideas:

• Spear a cheese cube with a cherry tomato and Spanish olive.
• Spear a marshmallow with a Maraschino cherry and a pineapple cube.
• Spear a ham cube with a pickle and a pineapple chunk.
• Spear a seedless grape with an apple chunk and mandarin orange section.
• Spear a green pepper square with a cucumber and mini-meatball.
• Any of your favorite luncheon meats will make good cold kabobs.

If you can't slice them up chunk style, form a chunk by making layers. Mix and match with fruits and vegetables. Plan ahead. Make several variations and store in a plastic bag in the refrigerator.

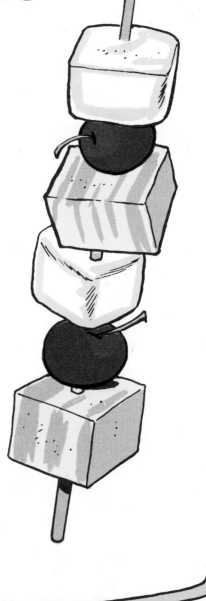

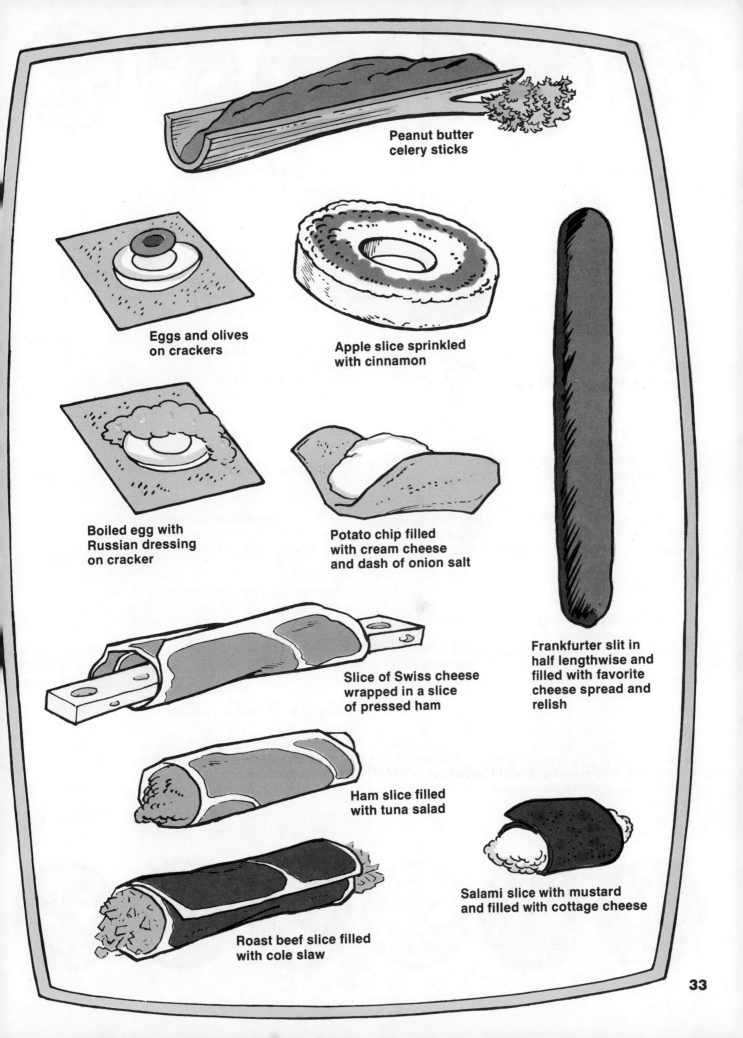

Peanut butter celery sticks

Eggs and olives on crackers

Apple slice sprinkled with cinnamon

Boiled egg with Russian dressing on cracker

Potato chip filled with cream cheese and dash of onion salt

Frankfurter slit in half lengthwise and filled with favorite cheese spread and relish

Slice of Swiss cheese wrapped in a slice of pressed ham

Ham slice filled with tuna salad

Salami slice with mustard and filled with cottage cheese

Roast beef slice filled with cole slaw

Franks and Ravioli

Serves 2

　　2 frankfurters, sliced diagonally
　　1 can (15 ounces) beef ravioli
　　2 teaspoons prepared mustard

Brown franks lightly in fry pan. Add ravioli and mustard; mix gently. Cook over low heat 5 to 10 minutes until mixture is thoroughly heated.

English Peanut Butter and Applesauce Muffins

Serves 2

　　peanut butter
　　applesauce
　　2 English muffins, split in half
　　4 slices American processed cheese, each slice cut into 4 strips

Spread each muffin half with peanut butter; then top with applesauce. Top with 2 thin strips of cheese in crisscross position. Place under broiler 3 minutes or until cheese melts. Serve hot.

Broiled Open-Faced Snacks

For each open sandwich, use buttered toasted bread or split English muffins. Then on each slice, arrange any of the following combinations. Place sandwich halves on cookie sheet or broiler pan. Broil about 6 inches from heat until bubbly or browned on top.

● Sliced frankfurters and Cheddar cheese strips
● Deviled ham sprinkled with grated Parmesan cheese
● Canned corned beef hash topped with thin onion rings
● Sliced cold roast beef or other sandwich meat with chili sauce
● Cheese slices, bacon slices, and barbecue sauce
● Bologna and tomato slices

Cocoa Crunchies

Makes 4 dozen

　　2 cups sugar
　　⅓ cup cocoa
　　¼ cup margarine
　　½ cup milk
　　3 cups quick oats, uncooked
　　1 cup crunchy peanut butter
　　2 teaspoons vanilla

In large saucepan, mix sugar and cocoa. Add margarine and milk. Bring to a boil. Let boil 2 minutes, stirring constantly. Remove from heat; add oats, peanut butter, and vanilla. Mix thoroughly. Drop by teaspoonfuls onto waxed paper. Let cool.

Orange Coconut Treats

Makes about 30

　　⅔ cup sweetened condensed milk
　　1⅓ cups flaked coconut
　　2 cans (1 pound each) mandarin orange sections

In bowl, combine milk and coconut. Mix well. Using tongs or fork, dip mandarin sections, one at a time, into coconut mixture until evenly coated. Place on waxed paper; let stand until firm.

Quick Raisin Pudding

Serves 2

　　2 cans (5 ounces each) vanilla pudding
　　2 tablespoons raisins
　　dash of nutmeg, cinnamon, or wheat germ

Open canned pudding. Mix 1 tablespoon of raisins into each can. Sprinkle on desired topping.

Bananas in Blankets

Serves 4

    1 tablespoon margarine
    4 ripe bananas, peeled
    ½ cup orange juice
    3 tablespoons powdered sugar
    6 slices bacon, cut in halves

Turn oven temperature to 350 degrees F. Grease baking pan with margarine. Cut bananas crosswise into thirds. Dip banana chunks in orange juice, roll in sugar, and wrap each section in ½ slice bacon. Fasten with a toothpick. Place in baking pan. Bake in oven for 10 minutes; turn and bake 10 minutes more or until bacon is crisp.

Quick Raisin Bread

Serves 1

    2 bread slices
    2 teaspoons raisins
    4 teaspoons pancake syrup

Place bread slices on dinner plate. Push raisins into bread. Make a design if you wish. Pour syrup on top and serve as an open sandwich.

Finger Toastees

Makes 30 strips

    1 tablespoon cinnamon
    ¼ cup sugar
    ½ loaf whole wheat bread
    ⅓ cup heavy cream
    3 tablespoons margarine

Turn oven temperature to 425 degrees F. In pie pan, combine cinnamon and sugar. Set aside. Remove crusts from bread slices. Cut each slice into 3 strips. Lightly grease 2 baking sheets. Dip each bread strip into cream; brush each side with margarine. Roll in cinnamon-sugar mixture. Place on baking sheets. Bake in oven for 20 minutes.

Toast Shells

Makes 8

    8 bread slices
    margarine
    favorite meat, vegetable, fish, or
    egg filling with sauce.

Turn oven temperature to 350 degrees F. Remove crust from bread slices. Spread margarine on each slice. Put a bread slice in each muffin pan cup with the buttered side down. Press the bread into the shape of the muffin cup. Bake in oven 20 minutes or until toast shells are light brown. When done, let cool on rack. Remove and fill each toast shell with your favorite food.

Party Stuffed Celery

Makes 12 sections

    4 celery stalks
    1 package (3 ounces) cream cheese,
      softened
    1 tablespoon tomato catsup
    3 tablespoons peanut butter

Wash and separate celery. Cut in twelve 3-inch pieces. In bowl, combine cream cheese, catsup, and peanut butter. Mix well until creamy. Stuff a little into each celery section. Place on serving tray; cover with plastic wrap and chill in refrigerator for 1 hour.

Party Stuffed Celery can be stuffed with many variations of your favorite goodies. Try tuna fish or egg or salmon or chicken salad or deviled ham spread.

KA-ZAR
STEAK KABOBS

Serves 4

- **1 pound round steak, cut into 1-inch cubes**
- **1 envelope meat marinade**
- **4 medium potatoes, cut into quarters**
- **2 green peppers, cut into large pieces favorite bottled barbecue sauce**

Cook potatoes until partially done. Follow manufacturer's instructions for making meat marinade mixture. Place meat and potatoes in marinade and coat. Let stand for 2½ hours. Alternate meat, potatoes, and peppers on skewers. Brush with barbecue sauce and broil 5 inches from heat for about 10 minutes. Turn and brush with sauce and cook 5 minutes longer.

Variations: You can make many variations of kabobs. Follow the recipe for Conan's Steak Kabobs and try these.

Pineapple Bobs. Instead of potatoes, alternate pineapple chunks. Use the syrup to brush bobs.

Mushroom and Tomato Bobs. Alternate fresh mushrooms and cherry tomatoes with meat cubes.

Onion and Apple Bobs. Alternate small onion balls and apple cubes with meat cubes.

THINK BIG!

SUPER MEAT LOAF "GOLIATH STYLE"

WOW! HALF A MEAT LOAF IS BETTER THAN NONE!

Super Meat Loaf

Serves 8

- 1 can (10½ ounces) condensed tomato soup
- 2 pounds ground beef
- 1 egg, slightly beaten
- ½ cup fine, dry breadcrumbs
- ½ cup chopped onion
- 1 tablespoon Worcestershire sauce
- 1 teaspoon salt
- 2 slices American processed cheese, cut into squares
  Spanish olives, sliced in half

Preheat oven to 350 degrees F. In large bowl, combine all ingredients except cheese and olives; mix well. Line loaf pan with foil. Place meat in pan and flatten top with pancake turner. (If you do not have a loaf pan, shape meat mixture into loaf and place in shallow baking pan.) Bake for about 1¼ hours.

When done, remove from oven. Let sit for 15 minutes. To drain off excess liquid from pan, press pancake turner on top of meat and carefully tilt loaf pan and spill out liquid; or liquid may be spooned out and discarded. Then remove meat from pan by gently lifting foil at sides, and place on dish. Top with cheese squares and sliced olives. Place in oven for 5 minutes or until cheese melts.

Porcupine Meatballs

Serves 4

¼ cup catsup
1 pound ground beef
¼ cup uncooked rice
1 egg, slightly beaten
½ teaspoon onion salt

2 tablespoons parsley flakes
1 teaspoon salt
1 can (8 ounces) tomato sauce
1 cup water

In bowl, combine all ingredients except tomato sauce and water. Shape into small balls about 1½ inches in diameter. Place in large frying pan; add tomato sauce and water. Cover and simmer over low heat about 45 minutes, stirring now and then.

Muffin Pan Meat Cakes

Makes 12 meat cakes

1 pound ground beef
½ teaspoon onion flakes
1 teaspoon salt

½ cup corn flakes
1 can (10½ ounces) vegetable soup

Preheat oven to 450 degrees F. In large bowl, combine all ingredients and mix thoroughly. Spoon into muffin pan cups; for easy removal from pan, meat mixture can be scooped into paper muffin cup liners. Bake for 15 minutes.

Pie Pan Meat Loaf

Serves 6

1½ pounds ground beef
1 can (8½ ounces) kidney beans
1 can (8½ ounces) tomato sauce
½ cup chopped pepper
½ cup chopped onion

1 teaspoon salt
1 egg, slightly beaten
1 cup packaged herb-seasoned stuffing

Preheat oven to 350 degrees F. In large bowl, combine all ingredients; mix thoroughly. Place in pie pan and smooth top. Bake for 1¼ hours.

Meat Loaf Squares

Serves 8

Follow recipe for Super Meat Loaf on page 40, but place meat mixture in square baking pan. Top with salted crackers, pimientos and olives.

THOR'S CABBAGE ROLLS

Serves 4

8 large cabbage leaves
1 pound ground beef
1 cup cooked rice
1 teaspoon onion flakes
1 egg, slightly beaten
1 teaspoon salt
1 can (10½ ounces) condensed tomato soup

Cook cabbage leaves in boiling salted water for a few minutes to soften; then drain onto paper towel. In bowl, combine beef, rice, onion flakes, egg, and salt. Add 4 tablespoons of soup. Lay out cabbage leaves and divide meat mixture onto each one. Roll leaves and secure with toothpicks. Place cabbage rolls in frying pan; pour remaining soup over all. Cover and cook over low heat for 40 minutes. Stir often, spooning soup over rolls.

DR. STRANGE'S MYSTERIOUS STEW

Serves 4

2 cans (10¾ ounces) beef bouillon
4 carrots, cut into small pieces
2 onions, chopped
3 ripe tomatoes, cut into quarters
2 medium-sized potatoes,
   pared and thinly sliced

½ teaspoon pepper
1 teaspoon salt
2 tablespoons margarine

In large pot, combine bouillon, carrots and potatoes. Cook over medium heat for 15 minutes. Add remaining ingredients and cook an additional 30 minutes.

A DAREDEVIL FAVORITE

"BE-DEVILED"
SWISS STEAK

Serves 4

- ¼ cup all-purpose flour
- 1½ pounds round steak (½ inch thick)
- 2 tablespoons salad oil
- 1 teaspoon salt
- 1 can (10½ ounces) condensed onion soup
- 4 medium carrots, cut into 2-inch pieces
- 4 medium potatoes, pared and cut in half
- 2 tablespoons parsley flakes

Place steak on a piece of waxed paper. Sprinkle flour over steak and pound in, using a meat hammer or the bottom of a heavy glass. Cut into 4 serving pieces. In large frying pan, heat salad oil; brown steak on both sides in oil. Add salt, soup, carrots, and potatoes. Cover; cook over low heat 45 minutes or until meat and vegetables are tender. Stir now and then. When done, sprinkle with parsley and serve hot.

SALUTE TO AMERICA'S BICENTENNIAL 1776-1976

MINUTEMEN STEAK AND FRIED ONIONS

Serves 4

flour
4 tablespoons margarine
2 large onions, peeled and sliced 1/4″ thick
4 minute steaks

Pour a little flour into a pie pan. Dip meat into flour and coat both sides. In frying pan, melt margarine over medium heat. Place onion strips in pan and cook for five minutes. Add steaks and fry one side 4 to 6 minutes, or until browned. Turn and fry other side 4 to 6 minutes. Stir onions in pan. When done, remove to serving plate and season with salt and pepper.

Onion rings are great to serve with Minutemen Steak. Buy the frozen packaged onion rings and follow the manufacturer's instructions. Use two frying pans for easier cooking — one for Minutemen Steak and the other for Onion Rings.

THE VISION

I'LL GO THRU ANY WALL FOR ONE OF THESE DISHES!

VEAL AND NOODLES

Serves 4

- 1 pound veal, thinly sliced
- 2 tablespoons flour
- 1 can (4 ounces) sliced mushrooms, drained
- ¼ cup margarine
- 1 teaspoon soy sauce
- 1 can (10½ ounces) condensed cream of celery soup
- ½ cup water
- 4 cups cooked noodles

Cut veal into 2-inch pieces. Spread a little flour on chopping board; pound into veal with meat hammer or edge of saucer. Heat margarine in frying pan. Brown veal. Add mushrooms, soy sauce, soup, and water; stir. Cover and cook over low heat 30 minutes or until meat is tender. Serve over noodles.

VEAL AND PEPPERS

Serves 4

- 1 pound veal, cut into 4-inch squares
- 1 teaspoon salt
- ½ teaspoon pepper
- ½ cup flour
- 3 tablespoons salad oil
- 3 large green peppers, thinly sliced
- 1 cup hot water
- ½ cup tomato sauce

Combine salt, pepper, and flour on chopping board. Pound into veal. Heat salad oil over medium heat. Brown meat on both sides. Add peppers; cover and sauté 10 minutes or until tender. Add water. Cover and simmer 20 minutes or until meat is done. Add tomato sauce and stir. Simmer 5 minutes longer.

DELICIOUS RECIPES TESTED IN THE ARENA OF THE DINNER TABLE AND FOUND MOST WORTHY!

KUNG FU CHICKEN

Serves 4

4 chicken breasts, whole
  salt and pepper
3 tablespoons salad oil
1 can (10 ounces) condensed cream of
  mushroom soup
1 can (16 ounces) meatless chow mein,
  drained
1 can (8¼ ounces) chunk pineapple

Preheat oven to 375 degrees F. Remove skin from chicken; season with salt and pepper. Heat oil in frying pan until hot; add chicken and brown on both sides. Place chicken in casserole dish; add soup. Bake in oven for 45 minutes. Combine chow mein and pineapple chunks in bowl. Pour over chicken and bake 15 minutes more. When done, remove from oven and stir soup, chow mein and pineapple mixture.

KUNG FU CHOP SUEY

Serves 4

1 can (10 ounces) condensed cream
  of celery soup
½ cup water
1 can (12 ounces) chop suey
  vegetables, drained
1½ cups diced cooked chicken
2 tablespoons soy sauce
2 cups cooked noodles
½ cup Chinese noodles

Preheat oven to 375 degrees F. In casserole dish, combine all ingredients except Chinese noodles. Bake in oven 25 minutes. When done, sprinkle Chinese noodles on top of casserole. Bake 5 minutes more.

BEEF LIVER WITH RICE

Serves 4

2 tablespoons margarine	1 medium onion, diced
1 pound sliced beef liver cut in 1-inch squares	1 can (8½ ounces) tomato sauce
¼ cup chopped green pepper	1 can (16 ounces) tomatoes
¼ cup chopped celery	1 teaspoon salt
	3 cups cooked rice parsley flakes

In large frying pan, melt margarine over low heat. Cook liver, pepper, celery, and onion until liver is lightly browned and vegetables are tender. Add tomato sauce, tomatoes, salt, and rice. Pour into greased 1½-quart casserole dish and bake at 350 degrees F for 25 minutes. When done, spread salt with parsley and serve hot.

CHICKEN LIVERS IN SHELLS Serves 4

2 strips bacon
½ pound fresh chicken livers
¼ cup chopped onion
1 can (10½ ounces) condensed cream of chicken soup
⅓ cup milk
¼ teaspoon paprika
4 patty shells

In frying pan, cook bacon until almost done. Add livers and onion; cook until tender turning livers often. Gradually blend in soup, milk, and paprika. Stir often. Place patty shells on serving dish. Spoon chicken liver mixture into each shell. (If shells are frozen, follow manufacturer's instructions for baking or thawing.)

3 QUICK AND EASY VARIATIONS

Tuna Muffin Pies

Serves 6

- 2 cans (10½ ounces) condensed cream of mushroom soup
- ¾ cup milk
- 2 cans (7 ounces) tuna, drained and flaked
- 1 can (16 ounces) peas and carrots, drained
  saltine crackers
- 12 toasted bread slices

Blend soup and milk; add tuna, peas and carrots. Heat; stir often. Place 2 saltine crackers in each cup of 12-cup muffin pan. Half-fill each cup with tuna mixture. Place toast on top and tuck in sides with fork. Bake in oven at 350 degrees F for 10 minutes. Use large spoon to scoop onto serving plate. Or, for extra convenience, make the pies in small foil baking pans, and serve in the pans.

Beef Pie

Serves 4

- 1 pound ground round steak
- 1 can (10¼ ounces) condensed vegetable soup
- 1 medium onion, finely chopped
- ½ cup shredded sharp Chedder cheese

Press meat against bottom and sides of 9-inch pie pan. Mix soup and onion; pour into meat shell. Bake in oven 40 minutes. Top with cheese and continue baking 10 minutes more or until cheese melts.

Chicken Pie

Serves 4 or 5

- 2 cups leftover cooked chicken, cut into small chunks
- 1 small green pepper, slivered
- 2 tablespoons chopped parsley
- 1 can (16 ounces) kernel corn
- 2 tablespoons margarine
- 2 tablespoons flour
- 1 can (10½ ounces) chicken broth
  salt and pepper
  pie pastry for one-crust pie (follow instructions on package for preparing)

Butter a 2-quart baking dish and fill with layers of chicken, green pepper, parsley, and corn, beginning and ending with a layer of chicken. In saucepan, melt margarine, stir in flour and cook for 2 minutes, stirring constantly. Add chicken broth and stir constantly until sauce thickens. Simmer for 5 minutes. Pour sauce over chicken and vegetables. Add salt and pepper. Cover with prepared pie crust; pierce holes in top of pie crust to allow steam to escape. Bake in hot oven (400 degrees) for about 20 minutes or until crust is browned.

Oven-Cooked Chicken

Serves 4

1 tablespoon margarine
¾ cup flour
1 teaspoon salt
1 teaspoon pepper

1 teaspoon paprika
2½ pounds chicken parts
½ cup melted margarine

Turn oven temperature to 325 degrees F. Grease a 2-quart casserole dish with margarine. In paper bag, combine flour, salt, pepper, and paprika. Place 1 chicken part at a time in the bag and shake to coat chicken. When coated, place in casserole dish. Pour melted margarine over chicken. Cover and bake in oven for 1 hour. Use tongs to turn chicken pieces and continue cooking without lid for 15 minutes more or until chicken is browned.

Chinese Chicken and Rice

Serves 4

3 cups cooked rice
1 can (10½ ounces) cream of mushroom soup
¼ cup milk
1½ cups cooked chicken or 2 cans (5 ounces) of boned chicken
1 can (16 ounces) chicken chow mein
1 tablespoon soy sauce

In large frying pan, combine soup and milk; stir. Add chicken, chow mein, and soy sauce; mix well. Cook over low heat about 15 minutes, stirring often. Serve over hot rice.

Peachy Baked Chicken

Serves 4

3 pound chicken, quartered
¼ cup tomato juice
⅓ cup lemon juice
½ teaspoon garlic powder

½ teaspoon salt
¼ teaspoon pepper
¼ pound melted margarine
1 can (16 ounces) peach halves

Remove skin from chicken. Place chicken pieces in casserole, flesh side up. In small bowl, blend tomato juice, lemon juice, garlic powder, salt, pepper, and melted margarine. Add liquid from peaches. Spoon this mixture over chicken pieces. Cover casserole with foil or lid and bake in oven, 350 degrees F, for 40 minutes, basting several times. Remove cover; add peaches and bake 15 minutes more.

Barbecued Chicken

Serves 4

    1 broiler-fryer, about 3 pounds,
       cut up
  ½ cup spaghetti sauce
  ¼ cup water
    1 teaspoon sugar

Turn oven temperature to 350 degrees F. Arrange chicken parts in shallow baking pan. Mix sauce, water, and sugar in bowl. Brush mixture on chicken. Bake in oven about 1 hour and 15 minutes, brushing spaghetti sauce mixture on chicken every 15 minutes.

Stewed Chicken

Serves 4

    2 pounds chicken parts
    1 can (10½ ounces) condensed cream of
       chicken soup
    1 cup water
    4 small carrots, cut into 2-inch pieces
    2 large stalks celery, cut into 2-inch pieces
    1 medium onion, thinly sliced

Combine chicken, soup, water, and vegetables in large heavy pan. Cover. Simmer over low heat about 40 minutes or until chicken is tender.

Southern Fried Chicken

Serves 4

    1 fryer chicken, 2½ pounds
  ½ cup all-purpose flour
 1½ teaspoons salt
  ½ teaspoon pepper
     salad oil (enough to fill large frying pan 1 to
     1½ inches deep)

Cut chicken in serving-size pieces and dry between paper towels. Combine flour and seasonings and use to coat chicken. Heat salad oil in large frying pan over medium heat. Place chicken parts in hot salad oil, skin side up, with thicker pieces near center. Cover and cook 10 to 15 minutes. When golden brown, turn; reduce heat. Finish cooking without lid. Turn again as needed. Chicken is done when easily pierced with fork. When done, remove chicken and drain on paper towels. Arrange chicken on hot platter and serve with your favorite vegetable and pasta.

Quick Chicken à la King

Serves 4

    1 can (10½ ounces) chicken à la
      king
    1 can (8 ounces) small green peas, drained
    1 can diced ham
    4 slices buttered toast, or 2 English muffins,
      split in half

In saucepan, combine all ingredients except toast or muffins. Heat, stirring now and then. Serve hot over toast or muffins.

FISH RECIPES

Salmon Loaf

Serves 4

- ½ teaspoon margarine
- 1 can (16 ounces) salmon
- 1 cup soft breadcrumbs
- 1 can (10½ ounces) condensed cream of celery soup
- 1 egg, slightly beaten
- ½ cup chopped onion
- ¼ cup chopped celery
- 1 teaspoon lemon juice

Turn oven temperature to 375 degrees F; grease loaf pan with margarine. Drain liquid from salmon into cup and save. Place salmon in bowl and use fork to remove skin; then flake. Add breadcrumbs and rest of ingredients; add salmon liquid. Mix well. Pour salmon mixture into loaf pan. Bake in oven 1 hour.

Tuna Fish Balls

Makes 1 dozen

- 1 package (3 ounces) cream cheese, softened
- 1 can (3¼ ounces) tuna
- 3 tablespoons parsley flakes
- ½ teaspoon onion salt

In bowl, mash cream cheese with fork. Drain oil from tuna and discard. Add tuna to cream cheese and mix thoroughly. Spread parsley flakes on chopping board. Sprinkle onion salt over parsley. Shape tuna mixture into small balls and roll in parsley flakes. Place on tray and chill in refrigerator until firm. Serve with potato chips, pickles, and sliced tomatoes.

Lemon-Baked Fish

Serves 4

- 1 tablespoon margarine
- 1 pound fish fillets
- 2 teaspoons lemon juice
- 1 teaspoon salt
- ½ teaspoon paprika
- 1 lemon, thinly sliced

Turn oven temperature to 325 degrees F. Grease baking dish with margarine. Place fish in baking dish. Sprinkle with lemon juice, salt and paprika. Arrange lemon slices on fish. Bake in oven 20 minutes or until fish is flaky when pierced with fork.

Variations: Omit lemon juice and lemon slices; pour tomato sauce, or a creamy sauce, or cheese sauce over fish before baking.

Deep-Fried Fish

Serves 4

- 1 pound fish fillets, fresh or frozen (¼'' thick)
- 1 egg, beaten
- 1 tablespoon milk
- ½ cup soft breadcrumbs
- 1 teaspoon salt
  salad oil for frying (enough to fill frying pan to ¾'' or to cover fish)

Dry fillets on paper towel. In a flat dish mix egg and milk. In pie pan, mix breadcrumbs and salt. Dip fish into egg mixture, then into breadcrumbs and salt. Dip fish into egg mixture, then into breadcrumb mixture. Heat salad oil over medium heat. Fry fish until golden brown, about 8 minutes. When done, use pancake turner to remove, and drain on paper towel.

SUB-MARINER

MAGNIFICENT TUNA BAKE

Serves 4

- 2 cans (7 ounces) tuna, drained and flaked
- 1 cup chopped celery
- 1 can (10¾ ounces) condensed cream of mushroom soup
- ¼ cup milk
- 2½ cups cooked noodles
- 1 can (8½ ounces) green peas, drained
- ½ cup breadcrumbs

Turn oven temperature to 350 degrees F. In 1½-quart casserole dish, blend soup and milk. Add remaining ingredients except breadcrumbs. Stir. Sprinkle breadcrumbs on top. Bake in oven 30 minutes.

HOLY TUNA!

HULK'S

JUMBO SHRIMP IN A BASKET

Serves 4

- 1 pound of boiled jumbo shrimp
- 1 cup milk
- 1 egg
- flour
- breadcrumbs
- salt
- pepper
- 1½ cups cooking oil

Clean shrimp. Combine milk and egg. Let stand for a few minutes. In pie pan, mix equal parts of flour and breadcrumbs with salt and pepper. Coat shrimp well with mixture. Heat oil in frying pan over medium heat. When oil is hot, use tongs to place shrimp in oil. Shrimp will rise to the top of hot oil when cooked. Use tongs to take out shrimp and place on paper towel. Serve with shrimp sauce or catsup.

A BARREL A DAY... KEEP DOCTOR AWAY!

SOMETHING FISHY HERE!

SPIDER-MAN's CATCH

Seafood Platter   Serves 8

1 package (12 ounces) frozen
   thin-cut French fries
2 packages (6 ounces) frozen deviled crab
1 package (6 ounces) frozen breaded shrimp
1 package (8 ounces) frozen fish sticks
1 package (8 ounces) frozen fish cakes
1 package (7 ounces) frozen, precooked
   breaded sea scallops
1 cup mayonnaise
2 tablespoons milk

Preheat oven to 425 degrees F. In large baking pan,
bake potatoes and crab 5 minutes. Add remaining
fish; bake 15 minutes more or until hot. Mix
mayonnaise and milk and serve with fish.

BLESS MY SOLE!

POWERMAN's FILLET OF SOLE

Serves 4

1 pound fresh whitefish fillets, or
   frozen fillets, thawed and blotted
   dry
1 can (10½ ounces) condensed tomato soup
   Parmesan cheese

In large baking pan, lay out fish. Stir soup in can
and pour over fish. Sprinkle Parmesan cheese on
top. Bake in oven set at 400 degrees F for 20
minutes.

DAREDEVIL's

DEVILED DIP

Makes 2¼ cups

1 package (8 ounces) cream
   cheese, softened
1 can (10½ ounces) condensed
   tomato soup
2 cans (4½ ounces each) deviled ham
2 tablespoons finely chopped green onion
¼ cup finely chopped cucumber

Beat cream cheese until smooth with electric
mixer or egg beater. Add remaining ingredients
and blend thoroughly. Chill. Serve with crackers, potato chips, or toast.

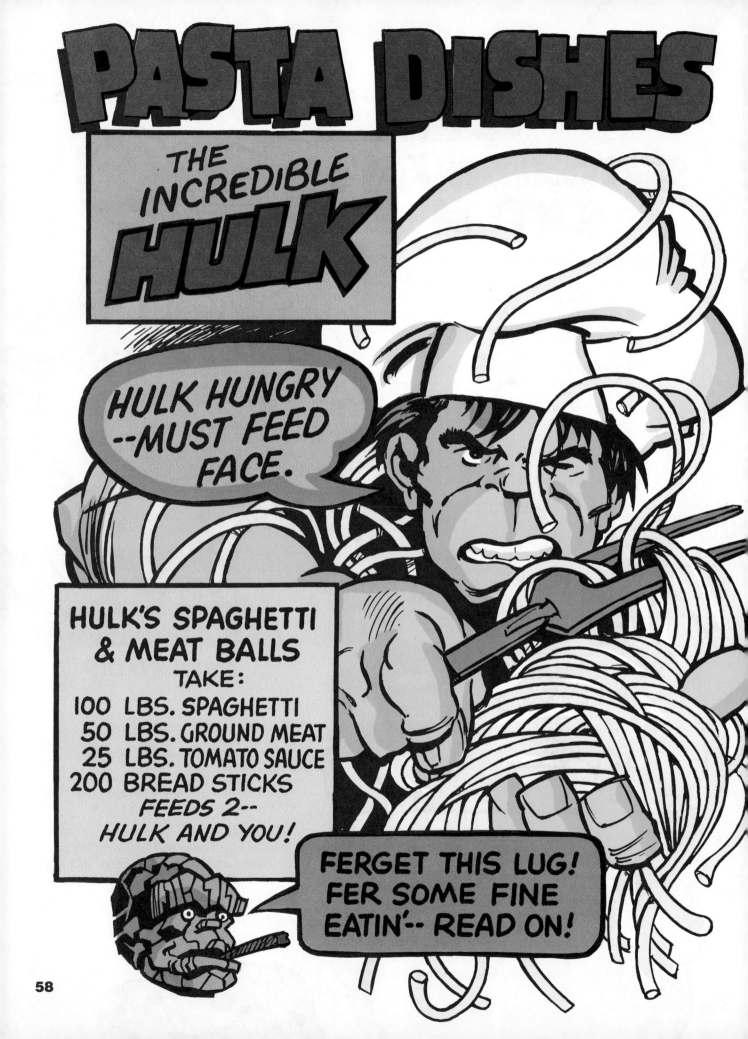

Pasta Plus

Spaghetti and Macaroni and Noodles belong to the Pasta family. The best basic recipe that you can follow for cooking these dishes is the label directions on the back of the package. Here are a few additional suggestions to help you.

● Make sure that the pot you are using is deep enough to hold the required amount of water. A pot that has handles or grips on both sides is especially convenient to use when emptying the water at the end of cooking time.
● After bringing water to a boil and adding the pasta of your choice, lower heat just enough to keep bubbles forming on top of water. Stir frequently so food doesn't stick to bottom.
● When done, place colander in sink. Carefully lift pot and pour contents into colander to drain.
● Hint: If getting the long sticks of spaghetti into boiling water is a problem, break them in half.

There are many dishes that you can make when you start with cooked pasta. It can be served by itself with sauce or combined with meats, fish, poultry, and vegetables. It can be used to stuff peppers, tomatoes, or cabbage rolls and can be served cold in salads.

Quick Macaroni and Chili Bean Dish   Serves 4

    2 cans (16 ounces) macaroni in cheese
      sauce
    2 cans (8½ ounces) chili beans
    1 tablespoon parsley flakes
      Parmesan cheese

Place macaroni and cheese in casserole dish. Mix in chili beans and parsley. Top with Parmesan cheese. Bake in oven at 350 degrees F for 15 minutes.

Spaghetti with Tuna   Serves 4

    ⅓ cup peanut oil
    ½ cup chopped green pepper
    ½ teaspoon onion flakes
    2 cans (7½ ounces) tuna fish, drained
      and flaked
    2 cans (8 ounces) tomato sauce
    ½ cup water
    1 teaspoon salt
    ½ teaspoon garlic powder
    1 package (8 ounces) thin spaghetti,
      cooked and drained
      Parmesan cheese

In large frying pan, heat oil. Add pepper; sauté until tender. Stir in onion flakes, tuna, tomato sauce, water, salt, and garlic powder. Cook over medium heat until thoroughly heated, about 8 minutes. Pour sauce over spaghetti. Sprinkle Parmesan cheese on top.

Hearty Yankee Noodle Bake
Serves 4

    6 frankfurters
    3 cups cooked noodles
    ¼ teaspoon onion salt
    1 can (10¾ ounces) tomato soup
    ½ cup water
    1 can (16 ounces) peas and carrots,
      drained

Slice frankfurters into 2-inch chunks. In casserole dish, combine all ingredients. Bake in oven 350 degrees F 25 minutes.

Lazy Lasagna   Serves 6

    2 jars (16 ounces) Marinara sauce
    8 ounces lasagna noodles, cooked
    1 pound cottage cheese
    8 ounces Mozzarella cheese, sliced
    ½ cup grated Parmesan cheese

Spread about ½ cup sauce in 13″ x 9″ x 2″ baking pan. Starting with noodles, make 3 layers each of noodles, cottage cheese, mozzarella, sauce, and Parmesan. Bake in preheated oven at 325 degrees F for 45 minutes.

QUICK COOK RICE

SHANG-CHI'S BASIC RICE RECIPE

Quick-cooking rice is available at the supermarket. It cooks in only a few minutes and is very easy to make. Follow the instructions on the package. But if you are *not* using quick-cooking rice, follow this basic recipe.

1 cup rice
2 cups cold water
¼ teaspoon salt
1 tablespoon butter or margarine

In saucepan, combine rice, water, salt, and butter or margarine. Bring to a boil. Lower heat to medium low. Stir with fork. Then cover pan and simmer 12 minutes or until all liquid is absorbed.

LOOK AT ALL THE NICE DISHES YOU CAN MAKE WITH RICE!

South-of-the-Border Rice

Serves 4

- 1 onion, chopped
- 1 pound ground beef
- 2 tablespoons salad oil
- 1 teaspoon salt
- 1 cup uncooked rice
- 2 cups tomato juice

In large frying pan, brown onion and beef in hot salad oil. Add rice and 1 cup tomato juice. Pour into greased casserole and bake in oven at 350 degrees F about 30 minutes, adding more tomato juice as it is absorbed.

Curried Rice and Peas

Serves 4

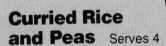

- 1 can (16 ounces) green peas, drained
- ¾ cup light cream
- ½ teaspoon curry powder
- 2 cups cooked rice
- 3 tablespoons margarine
- ¼ teaspoon salt

In saucepan, combine all ingredients and cook over medium heat about 10 minutes or until hot.

Chinese Browned Rice

Serves 4

- 3 tablespoons margarine
- 1⅓ cups quick-cooking rice
- 1¼ cups water
- 2 tablespoons soy sauce
- ½ cup raisins

Melt margarine in saucepan. Add rice and cook over medium heat until golden brown, stirring constantly. Add water, soy sauce, and raisins. Quickly bring to a boil. Cover and remove from heat. Let stand 5 minutes. Fluff with fork and serve hot.

Vegetable Rice

Serves 4

- 1 can (8 ounces) mixed vegetables
- 1 can (8 ounces) stewed tomatoes
- 2 cups cooked rice
- 1 teaspoon soy sauce

Use strainer to drain liquid from vegetables. Pour tomatoes into frying pan. Mix in rice, vegetables, and soy sauce. Stir; cook over low heat about 10 minutes, stirring occasionally. Serve hot.

Rice and Beef Dish

Serves 4

- 1 pound ground beef
- 1 tablespoon margarine
- ¼ cup diced onion
- 2 teaspoons salt
- 1 can (16 ounces) tomatoes, drained
- 1 can (12 ounces) kernel corn, drained
- 1 bouillon cube dissolved in 1½ cups boiling water
- 1½ cups quick-cooking rice

In large frying pan, melt margarine. Add meat and brown quickly over medium heat. Add onion; cook until onion is tender. Add salt, tomatoes, corn, and bouillon; bring to boil. Stir in rice. Lower heat; cover and simmer 5 minutes. When done, fluff with fork.

VEGETABLES AND SALADS

Vegetables and salads are valuable foods because of the vitamins and minerals they supply. They should be included in everyone's daily meal planning.

Hulk Hints:

• Always wash fresh vegetables to remove any dust or sand that may have gathered on the skin or outer leaves.
• When cooking vegetables, use as little water as possible.
• Do not overcook vegetables. Important vitamins can be lost.

How to Cook Fresh Vegetables:

Place vegetables in small amount of boiling water. Cover and let water come to a boil again. Lower heat and cook until tender without stirring. Watch vegetables carefully while cooking to prevent them from burning. If the water evaporates before the vegetables are cooked, start all over again with freshly boiled water and continue cooking until done. When a vegetable can be easily pierced with a fork, it is done.

How to Cook Frozen Vegetables:

It is best to follow label directions on the back of the package. Be sure that the pan is large enough for the frozen vegetables to lie flat.

How to Cook Canned Vegetables:

Canned vegetables have already been cooked, so you only have to heat them. Drain the liquid from the can into a saucepan and bring quickly to a boil. Then add the vegetables and cook over low heat 3 or 4 minutes.

Boiled Potatoes

Serves 4

    6 medium-sized potatoes
    1 tablespoon salt

Wash and pare potatoes. Place in pot of boiling water, enough to cover potatoes. Cook for 25 minutes or until tender. Add salt. Drain and serve hot.

Mashed Potatoes

Serves 4

    6 medium-sized potatoes
  1½ cups water
    1 teaspoon salt
   ⅓ cup milk
    3 tablespoons butter

Wash and pare potatoes. Cut into quarters. Pour water into pot; add potatoes and salt. Let potatoes boil for 25 to 30 minutes or until tender when pierced with fork. Drain water from pot. Mash potatoes with fork. Add milk and butter; mash again. For softer consistency, add more milk while mashing.

French Fried Potatoes

Serves 4

    4 medium-sized potatoes
    4 tablespoons margarine
   ½ teaspoon salt
   ¼ teaspoon pepper

Pare and wash potatoes. Cut into lengthwise strips. Melt margarine in frying pan; add potato strips and sprinkle with salt and pepper. Cover and cook over medium heat for 10 minutes. Turn with pancake turner; cover and cook 10 minutes until crisp. Drain on paper towel.

Quick Sweet Potato Bake

Serves 4

    1 tablespoon margarine
    1 can (16 ounces) sweet potatoes
    1 can (14 ounces) cinnamon apple slices
    2 teaspoons brown sugar
   ½ teaspoon salt
    2 tablespoons butter

Turn oven temperature to 350 degrees F. Grease large baking dish with margarine. Drain liquid from sweet potatoes and apples. Cut potatoes into 2-inch slices. Place a layer of potatoes in bottom of baking dish. Place a layer of apple rings on top. Place remaining potatoes on top. Place a layer of remaining apple rings on top. Sprinkle brown sugar and salt over all and dot with butter. Cover and bake for 30 minutes.

Note: For a juicier Sweet Potato Bake, reserve the liquid from the apple rings and pour over all before putting on brown sugar and salt.

Fried Tomato Slices

Serves 4

    4 medium-sized tomatoes
   ¼ cup margarine
   ¾ cup fine breadcrumbs
    1 can (10½ ounces) condensed cream of
      mushroom soup
   ⅓ cup milk

Slice tomatoes in thin slices. Melt margarine in large frying pan. Spread breadcrumbs on a dinner plate. Dip tomato slices in breadcrumbs, coating them. Place breaded tomato slices in frying pan and cook over low heat until lightly browned; turn with pancake turner and brown other side. Remove tomatoes to dinner plate. Pour soup and milk into frying pan and heat for 5 minutes, stirring constantly. Pour sauce over tomatoes and serve hot.

Corn on the Cob
Serves 4

    4 ears of corn
    water
    1 tablespoon honey or pancake syrup
    butter or margarine
    salt and pepper

Remove husks (leaves) and silks (threads) from corn. Half-fill large pot with water. Bring to a boil. Add honey or syrup. Place corn in boiling water. If water in pot is too high and there is a chance that it will boil over, scoop some out with a cup. Cover pot and let corn boil about 8 to 10 minutes or until tender. When done, use tongs to remove corn from pot. Serve hot with butter or margarine, salt, and pepper.

Asparagus Parmesan
Serves 4

    2 tablespoons melted margarine
    2 cans (1 pound) asparagus
      salt and pepper
    ⅓ cup dry breadcrumbs
    2 tablespoons Parmesan cheese

Turn oven temperature to 375 degrees F. Grease 1-quart casserole dish or small baking pan with margarine. Drain liquid from asparagus. Place asparagus in baking dish. Sprinkle with salt and pepper. In bowl, mix breadcrumbs and margarine; sprinkle over asparagus. Top with Parmesan cheese. Bake in oven for 20 minutes.

Baked Tomatoes and Cheese
Serves 4

    2 large tomatoes, cut into halves
    1 tablespoon Parmesan cheese, or
      2 slices American processed cheese
    1 tablespoon bacon bits

Turn oven temperature to 400 degrees F. Place tomato halves in foil-lined pie pan, cut side up. Sprinkle on cheese and bacon bits. (If using American cheese, cut each slice in half and place on top of tomato.) Bake in oven 10 minutes.

Buttered Carrots
Serves 4

    4 carrots
    ½ teaspoon salt
    margarine

Wash carrots. Remove skins if you wish. Cut carrots into strips or slices or large chunks. Fill saucepan ¼ full with water. Heat to boiling over medium-high heat. Add carrots and salt. Cover pan. Lower heat as soon as water starts to boil again. Boil gently 15 minutes or until carrots are tender. When done, drain and add margarine. Serve hot.

Quick Glazed Carrots
Serves 2

    1 can (16 ounces) whole carrots
    ¼ cup honey
    1 tablespoon margarine

Drain liquid from canned carrots. In frying pan, heat honey and margarine over low heat. Add carrots; cook for 10 minutes, turning to coat all sides of carrots.

You can use this honey and margarine mixture to glaze sweet potatoes, frankfurters, sausages, or cooked corn on the cob.

Spinach Italian
Serves 4

    1½ pounds fresh or frozen spinach
      (if frozen, follow label directions for
      preparation)
    1 teaspoon lemon juice
    1 can (8 ounces) tomato sauce
      parmesan cheese

Place spinach in large, deep pot. Fill pot with water and wash spinach. Change water a few times to remove all sand. Pick out and discard roots and tough stems. Place spinach on paper towel to drain. Put spinach in pot and fill with enough water to cover leaves. Cover and cook 8 to 10 minutes or until tender. Stir occasionally with fork. Meanwhile, heat tomato sauce; add lemon juice. When spinach is done, place in colander in sink to drain. Stir in tomato sauce. Serve hot topped with Parmesan cheese.

FOUR FANTASTIC VEGETABLE DISHES

MORE!

P.S. THIS EPISODE SHOULD ILLUSTRATE THE DELICIOUSNESS OF TASTY COOKED VEGETABLES.

ZANGY CASSEROLES

Mixed-Up Casserole Dish
Serves 4

2 tablespoons margarine
4 celery stalks, cut into 2-inch chunks
2 medium-sized onions, thinly sliced
2 cans (16 ounces) baby carrots, drained
1 can (16 ounces) green string beans, drained
1 can (11 ounces) condensed Cheddar cheese soup
¼ cup milk

In frying pan, melt margarine and sauté celery chunks until tender. Place onions, carrots, and string beans in shallow baking dish. Add celery. Blend soup and milk; pour over top and stir. Bake in oven at 350 degrees F for 25 minutes.

MORE VITALITY COMING UP! AND UP! AND UP!

Spinach and Corn Casserole Serves 4

    2 packages (10 ounces each) frozen
      spinach, cooked and drained
    1 can (16 ounces) whole kernel corn
    2 cups diced ham
    1 can (10½ ounces) condensed cream of
      celery soup
    ⅓ cup milk
      crushed peanuts

Place a layer of spinach on the bottom of a 1½-quart casserole dish. Combine corn, ham, soup, and milk and blend. Pour over spinach. Top with crushed peanuts. Bake in oven at 375 degrees F for 30 minutes.

Grilled Tomato with Cheese

Serves 4

    4 tomatoes
      salt
    4 slices American processed cheese

Cut tomatoes into halves; sprinkle with salt. Broil 5 inches from heat at 350 degrees F for about 10 minutes. Place cheese slices on top of tomato halves. Turn oven off and let tomatoes remain in oven about 5 minutes or until cheese is partially melted.

Stuffed Peppers

Serves 4

    4 green peppers
    1 cup of minced cooked meat (chicken, ham,
      ground beef)
    1 cup moistened breadcrumbs
    ½ teaspoon salt
    1 tablespoon margarine

Cut a slice from stem end of each pepper. Remove seeds; parboil peppers 10 minutes. In bowl, mix meat, breadcrumbs, salt, and margarine. Stuff peppers with mixture and place in baking pan. Add water. Bake in oven at 375 degrees F for 30 minutes. Spoon water over peppers frequently.

Variations: Stuff peppers with cooked macaroni or rice or spaghetti. Vegetables are an excellent filler topped with cheese or tomato sauce.

SALADS

Greens are the start of almost all salads, lettuce being the most popular. A lettuce leaf holding fruit or tomatoes or eggs or cheese or any meat-salad mixture or a combination of any of these is simple to prepare and delicious to serve.

- Always wash and dry salad greens thoroughly before using. This makes the dressing cling to the leaves.
- Always break greens; do not cut them.
- Store greens in a covered bowl in refrigerator.
- Add moist ingredients and dressing just before serving.

Iron Man's Special Salad

Serves 4

- 2 cups chicken or turkey or ham, cut up
- 2 tomatoes, cut in wedges
- 1 cup sliced celery
- 1 small cucumber, thinly sliced
- 1 small onion, thinly sliced
- ¼ cup chopped green pepper
- ½ cup sour cream
  salt and pepper to taste
  lettuce
- 2 hard-cooked eggs, sliced

In large serving bowl, combine all ingredients except lettuce and eggs; stir. Serve on crisp lettuce leaves. Top with egg slices.

Lettuce and Tomato Salad

Serves 2

- 1 ripe red tomato
- 4 lettuce leaves
  dressing

Wash tomato; cut into thin slices. Place two lettuce leaves on each serving plate. Arrange tomato slices on top of lettuce. Spoon on dressing. You may add any of the following foods to the salad: carrot sticks, chopped tuna, salmon, diced luncheon meat, cottage cheese, olives, pickle, or relish. Anything goes with lettuce and tomatoes.

Tossed Green Salad

Serves 4

- ½ head lettuce
- 2 celery stalks
- 1 carrot
- ¼ cup French dressing, or your choice of other favorites
  croutons (optional)

Wash and dry lettuce and celery. Cut off ends and tips of celery stalks and discard. Cut celery into small pieces. Pare carrot and cut into penny slices. Tear lettuce into small pieces and place in salad serving bowl. Add celery and carrots; toss together with fork. Pour dressing over salad and toss again to coat all ingredients. Top with croutons. Using this basic recipe, you can add any of your favorite vegetables or fruits — fresh or canned. If using canned items, drain off liquid.

Chicken Salad   Serves 4

2 cups diced chicken
1 cup diced celery
½ cup mayonnaise
   salt and pepper
4 large lettuce leaves

Combine chicken, celery, and mayonnaise; mix well. Season with salt and pepper. Serve on lettuce leaf or make sandwiches.

Mixed Vegetable Salad   Serves 2

½ cup diced celery
1 can (8½ ounces) peas and carrots, drained
1 tablespoon French dressing
2 lettuce leaves

Combine celery with peas and carrots; mix in dressing. Serve equal portions on lettuce leaves.

Tuna Macaroni Salad   Serves 4

3 cups cooked elbow macaroni
2 cans (3¾ ounces) tuna, drained and flaked
½ cup green pepper strips
1 teaspoon onion salt
   French dressing

In bowl, toss all ingredients. Serve on crisp salad greens.

Ham and Egg Salad   Serves 4

2 tablespoons mayonnaise
1 cup celery, finely diced
2 teaspoons vinegar
1 cup diced, cooked ham (or favorite luncheon meat)
3 hard-cooked eggs, chopped

Stir mayonnaise into celery in large bowl. Add vinegar and blend. Toss in ham and mix; add chopped eggs.

Deviled Ham Salad   Serves 2

2 hard-cooked eggs
1 can (3½ ounces) deviled ham spread
3 tablespoons mayonnaise
½ teaspoon onion salt
2 lettuce leaves

Put eggs and deviled ham in bowl. Mash with fork. Add other ingredients and mix well. Serve on lettuce leaf or make sandwiches.

Egg Salad   Serves 2

2 hard-cooked eggs
1 teaspoon parsley flakes
2 tablespoons mayonnaise
4 large potato chips
2 lettuce leaves

Put eggs, parsley flakes, and mayonnaise in bowl; mash with fork until mixed. Crumble potato chips and sprinkle over egg mixture. Stir mixture. Place on lettuce leaf or make sandwiches.

CAKE BAKE

Cake mixes are convenient to use and are good tasting. Always follow the label directions carefully. For variety, you can add crushed peanuts, raisins, small fruit pieces, or coconut to the batter. To make a one-layer cake without a mix, follow this recipe. To make two layers, double the amount of ingredients.

One-Layer Cake

Makes 1 9-inch layer cake

> 1 tablespoon margarine
> 1 cup sifted flour
> ½ cup sugar
> ½ teaspoon baking powder
> 1 egg
> ¼ cup butter or margarine, softened
> ¼ cup milk
> ½ teaspoon vanilla extract (optional)

Preheat oven to 375 degrees F. Grease cake pan with margarine. In large bowl, sift flour, sugar, and baking powder. In second bowl, combine egg, butter or margarine, milk, and vanilla. Mix well. Add this mixture to the flour mixture; mix well. Pour mixture into cake pan. Bake in oven 25 minutes.

COOL IT!

Use pot holders to remove cake pans from oven. Cool cakes on a wire rack for 10 minutes.

When cake is cooled, circle a butter knife around the rim of cake pan to loosen cake.

To remove cakes from pan, place a second wire rack on top of cake, holding racks together as illustrated. Carefully turn the cake over. Lift the pan from the cake. To turn the cake right side up, place a wire rack over bottom of cake and, holding racks together, turn cake to right side as illustrated.

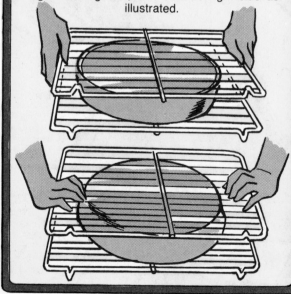

Superheroes' FROSTINGS

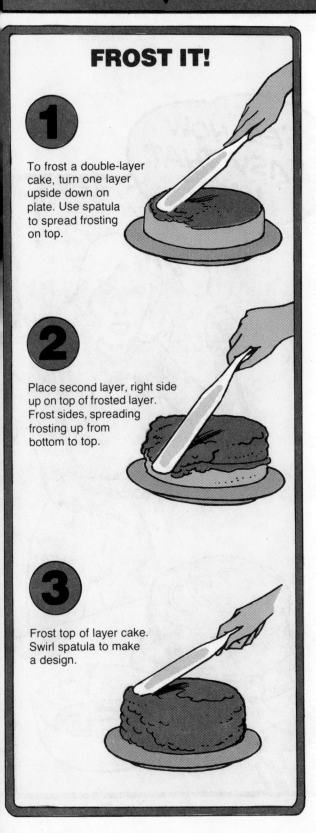

FROST IT!

1

To frost a double-layer cake, turn one layer upside down on plate. Use spatula to spread frosting on top.

2

Place second layer, right side up on top of frosted layer. Frost sides, spreading frosting up from bottom to top.

3

Frost top of layer cake. Swirl spatula to make a design.

The following frosting recipes are for double-layer cakes. For frosting a single-layer cake, divide the amounts in half.

Real Chocolate Frosting
Enough to frost double-layer cake

- 1 cup sugar
- ¾ cup evaporated milk
- 4 (1-ounce) squares unsweetened chocolate, cut into chunks
- ¼ teaspoon vanilla extract

Put all ingredients in the container of blender. Operate blender at low speed for 5 seconds. Then switch to high speed and blend for 3 or 4 minutes or until frosting thickens. Turn blender off. Scoop out frosting with tablespoon and frost cakes.

Chocolate Whipped Cream
Frosts 9-inch single-layer cake

- 1 pint heavy cream
- 1 cup sifted confectioners' sugar
- ½ cup sifted unsweetened cocoa

Pour cream into bowl. Beat with an egg beater until it starts to thicken. Sift sugar and cocoa into the cream, a little at a time. Continue beating until thick enough to spread.

White Frosting Makes ¾ cup

- 1 cup sifted confectioners' sugar
- 4 teaspoons milk
- ¼ teaspoon vanilla extract

In bowl, mix all ingredients until creamy.

Quick Fluffy Frosting Makes 1½ cups

- 1 egg white
- ½ cup honey

In bowl, beat egg white with egg beater until stiff enough to stand in peaks. Slowly pour honey in while beating constantly until frosting holds its shape. Spread on cake.

Lemon-Orange Sauce Makes 1 cup

- 1 cup orange juice
- ½ cup sugar
- 2 tablespoons cornstarch
- 1 tablespoon lemon juice

Put all ingredients into container of blender. Cover and blend on low speed for 20 seconds. Turn off blender and pour contents into saucepan and cook over low heat until thickened, stirring constantly. Serve hot.

No-Cook Chocolate Frosting

Enough to frost two 9-inch layers

   ½ cup margarine
   4 cups sifted sugar
   ½ cup cocoa
   ½ cup undiluted evaporated milk
   1½ teaspoons vanilla extract

In bowl, blend margarine, sugar, cocoa, milk, and vanilla. Mix with electric beater until smooth and creamy.

Strawberry-Coconut Sauce

Makes 1 cup

   1 package (10 ounces) frozen strawberries
   2 tablespoons sugar
   4 tablespoons flaked coconut

Put all ingredients into container of blender and cover. Blend at high speed for 20 seconds. Turn off blender. Pour mixture into strainer and strain into bowl. Refrigerate until ready to serve. Serve over ice cream, pound cake, pancakes, or puddings.

Peanut Butter Frosting

Enough to frost two 9-inch layers

   1 package (15 ounces) creamy white frosting mix
   ¾ cup creamy peanut butter
   ½ cup hot water

Mix together frosting mix, peanut butter, and ¼ cup water in large bowl until blended. Add remaining ¼ cup water and beat until smooth.

Butter Cream Frosting

Frosts two 8-or 9-inch layers

   1 package (1 pound) confectioners' sugar, sifted
   ⅓ cup soft margarine
   ¼ cup milk
   1 teaspoon vanilla extract

In blender container, combine all ingredients. Blend at medium speed for 1½ minutes. Turn off blender. Scoop out frosting with rubber spatula. If frosting is too stiff, add 2 tablespoons milk and stir.

Fudge Topping

Makes 1½ cups

   ½ cup chocolate syrup
   ½ cup chunk-style peanut butter
   ½ cup light corn syrup

Mix thoroughly chocolate syrup and peanut butter. Add corn syrup, stirring until well blended. Spoon on ice cream or dessert.

Sugar Glaze

Glazes one 9-inch layer cake

   ½ cup confectioners' sugar
   ¼ cup water
   ½ teaspoon vanilla extract

Put all ingredients into a small bowl and blend with a spoon until creamy. Pour the glaze on top of your cake, fruit tarts, or cupcakes, and let it sit for 1 hour before serving.

MS. FANTASTIC SHORT CAKES

GUARANTEED TO BECOME INVISIBLE UPON SERVING!

Quick Strawberry Shortcake

Serves 4

- 4 thin slices white bread*
- 4 tablespoons margarine
- 1 package (14 ounces) frozen strawberries, thawed
- 4 tablespoons sugar
  prepared whipped cream topping

Trim crusts from bread. In large frying pan, melt margarine. Lightly brown bread slices. Remove bread slices and place on serving dishes. In bowl, mix strawberries with sugar. Pile strawberries on top of bread. Top each serving with whipped cream.
*For Super Strawberry Shortcake, substitute pound cake for bread.

Jelly Cakes   Serves 2

- 4 slices pound cake
- 4 tablespoons jelly
  whipped cream

Spread jelly on each of 2 pound cake slices. Place second slices on top. Cut into 4 pieces. Top with whipped cream.

Raisin Bread Short Cake

Serves 2

- 4 slices bread
  raisins
  pancake syrup
  ice cream

Trim crusts from bread; place bread slices on plate. Push raisins into bread creating a design. Place a scoop of ice cream on top and pour on syrup.

Fruited Short Cakes
From a Single Layer Cake

Serves 6

- 1 single-layer cake, cut into 6 pieces, or store-bought cake
  your favorite fruit, cut into slices
  maraschino cherries
  whipped cream
  coconut

Prepare single-layer cake. Place fruit slices on top. Dot with cherries. Add whipped cream and top with coconut.

DARE DEVIL'S FOOD CAKE

Makes two 8- or 9-inch layers

1 package devil's food cake mix
miniature marshmallows
½ cup crushed peanuts

Preheat oven to 350 degrees F. Prepare mix according to label directions. Pour into baking pans. Place marshmallows around the outer circle as illustrated. Sprinkle peanuts on top. Bake in oven 35 minutes. This cake is so good, you don't have to frost it!

HULK'S APPLESAUCE CAKE

Makes one 13″ x 9″ cake

1 tablespoon margarine
1 package applesauce cake mix
¼ cup molasses
1 cup chopped nuts
canned vanilla frosting

Preheat oven to 350 degrees F. Grease loaf baking pan with margarine. In large bowl, prepare cake mix according to label directions. Add molasses and chopped nuts: mix. Pour into baking pan and bake in oven 35 to 40 minutes. When done, let cool. Spread frosting on top.

IRON MAN'S PEACHY CAKE

Makes one 13″ x 9″ cake

2 tablespoons margarine
1 package white cake mix
½ cup water
2 cups sliced peaches, drained
whipped-cream topping

Preheat oven to 375 degrees F. Grease bottom and sides of baking pans. In bowl prepare cake mix according to label directions; add water. Stir in peaches. Pour into baking pan. Bake in oven 35 minutes. Serve warm topped with whipped cream.

THE ANGEL'S HEAVENLY ANGEL CAKE

Makes two 8- or 9-inch layers

1 package angel food cake mix
1 can (1 pound) red pitted cherries
2 tablespoons cornstarch
½ cup sugar
2 tablespoons lemon juice

Prepare angel food cake mix and bake according to label directions. When done, let cool. Drain juice from cherries into saucepan. Stir in cornstarch, sugar, and lemon juice. Mix in cherries. Cook over medium heat until thickened, about five minutes, stirring occasionally. Serve warm over sliced Heavenly Angel Cake.

CAKES!

CAPTAIN AMERICA'S DOUBLE CRACKER JACK CAKE

Makes two 8- or 9-inch layers

> 2 single-layer cakes
> chocolate frosting
> Cracker Jacks

Spread frosting between layers and cover sides and top. Scatter Cracker Jacks on top and gently press down into frosting.

SPIDEY'S VANILLA CHEESE CAKE

Makes one 8- inch cake

> 1 8- or 9-inch graham cracker pie crust (page 86)
> 1 package (8 ounces) cream cheese
> 1 package (3¾ ounces) French vanilla mix-and-serve pudding

Prepare pie shell according to directions on page 86. Put cream cheese into bowl; stir until very soft. Add ½ cup milk and stir. Add remaining milk and pudding mix; beat slowly with egg beater for 1 minute. Pour into pie crust. Chill in refrigerator 1 hour.

SHANG-CHI'S PEACHES-AND-CREAM CAKE

Serves 6

> ½ package (8 ounces) butterscotch cake mix
> ¾ cup dairy sour cream
> 1 can (1 pound) sliced peaches, drained
> 2 tablespoons brown sugar

Prepare half of cake mix* following label directions. Bake and let cool. Spread sour cream over layer and arrange well-drained peach slices on top. Sprinkle with sugar; set under broiler 4 to 5 inches from heat source. Broil 5 minutes or until sugar melts and peaches brown on edges.

*Make two cakes by doubling the ingredients except for cake mix.

DR. STRANGE'S CINNAMON RAISIN BARS

Makes 2 dozen

> 1 cup seedless raisins
> 1 cup water
> ½ cup salad oil
> 1 cup sugar
> 1 egg, slightly beaten
> 1¾ cups enriched flour
> 1 teaspoon cinnamon

Preheat oven to 375 degrees F. In saucepan, combine raisins and water; bring to a boil. Turn off heat. Stir in salad oil and let stand 5 minutes. Stir in sugar and egg. Add flour and cinnamon; beat into mixture. Pour into greased 13″ x 9″ x 2″ baking pan. Bake 20 minutes or until done. When cool, cut into bars.

Cake mixes can be used to make cupcakes. Follow the instructions on the box carefully to get the best results. Most packages will indicate how many cupcakes you can make. However, if you do not find it, use this as your guide:

1 package (18½ ounces) will make 24 cupcakes. If you divide the ingredients in half, the yield will be 12 cupcakes.

• Preheat oven to 350 degrees.
• Use paper muffin pan liners or grease muffin pan with shortening.
• In bowl, combine all ingredients. Beat with egg beater until fairly smooth.
• Fill muffin pan cups half full.
• Bake in oven 25 minutes or according to manufacturer's directions.
• When done, let stand a few minutes before removing from pan. From a basic mix, you can make many different variations. Add or mix in any of the following just before you pour the batter into the muffin pans.

Banana Cupcakes

Peel 1 ripe banana and cut into penny slices. Mix into batter.

Peanut Butter Cupcakes

Mix 3 tablespoons of peanut butter into batter.

Raisin Cupcakes

Stir in ½ cup raisins into batter.

Marshmallow Cupcakes

Place a few miniature marshmallows on top of batter in muffin pan before putting into oven.

Fruited Cupcakes

Fill muffin pan cups a quarter full. Place a thin slice of canned fruit (peach, pineapple, pear, mandarin section) on top of batter. Top with 2 tablespoons of batter. Bake in oven.

Toppings can turn any cupcake into a masterpiece. Try some of these ideas and make up some of your own.

1. White frostings with colorful candies placed on top.
2. Divide cupcake by spreading chocolate frosting on one half and white frosting on the other half.
3. Whipped cream cupcake topped with a strawberry.
4. Top cupcake with jelly beans or peanuts.
5. Whipped cream cupcake topped with coconut flakes.
6. Any kind of frosting on a cupcake topped with multicolored sprinkles.
7. Lemon pudding spread on a cupcake with candies for eyes, licorice for mouth and a grape or strawberry for the nose.
8. A goodie all by itself ... the chocolate cupcake (see below).
9. Banana cupcake with raisins on top.
10. Spread jam or jelly on top of cupcake.
11. Chocolate frosting spread topped with miniature marshmallows.

Chocolate Cup Cakes

Serves 12

> 1 package (16 ounces) fudge brownie mix
> 2 eggs
> ¼ cup water

Turn oven temperature to 350 degrees F. Line muffin pan cups with paper lines, or grease entire cup with margarine or butter. In large bowl, combine brownie mix, eggs, and water. Beat with egg beater or electric mixer until smooth. Fill each muffin cup two-thirds full. Bake in oven for 25 minutes. Remove and place on rack to cool.

Packaged muffin mixes are convenient and easy to make. But making muffins is not the same as making cupcakes, although the instructions on the back of the package may read the same. When blending, the batter should be slightly lumpy and blended only until the dry ingredients are thoroughly moistened.

Basic Recipe

Makes 12 muffins

2 cups of all-purpose flour
¼ cup sugar
3 teaspoons baking powder
1 teaspoon salt
¼ cup vegetable oil
1 egg, slightly beaten
1 cup milk

In large bowl, stir in flour, sugar, baking powder and salt. Add oil and stir so that batter resembles coarse crumbs. In second bowl, combine egg and milk. Add to flour mixture; stir just until moistened. Batter will be lumpy. Line muffin cups with paper cup liners or grease with margarine. Spoon in batter until muffin cup is ⅔ full. Bake in oven at 400 degrees for 25 minutes.

You can vary the taste of muffins by adding any one of the following to the egg and milk mixture. Then proceed as instructed.

Onion Muffins

Add ½ cup finely chopped onion to milk and egg mixture.

Cheese Muffins

Add ½ cup shredded sharp Cheddar cheese to egg and milk mixture.

Jelly Muffins

Fill muffin cups half full of batter. Drop a teaspoon of jelly in center of batter. Then add a tablespoon more batter on top to fill muffin cup ⅔ full. Bake as instructed.

Using the above suggestion, you can create many other recipes. Center your muffin with cut-up ham or cheese or meat slices or spreads. Use frankfurters cut into penny slices for a delicious treat. There is no end to what you can add. Just remember that the muffin cup should be only ⅔ full.

Raisin Cookies

Makes 30 cookies

- 1 tablespoon margarine
- 1 can (16 ounces) sweetened
  condensed milk
- 3 tablespoons peanut butter
- 2 cups raisins

Preheat oven to 375 degrees F. Grease cookie sheet with margarine. In bowl, mix together milk, peanut butter, and raisins. Drop mixture by teaspoonfuls onto cookie sheet. Bake in oven for 12 minutes or until browned. When done, remove at once from cookie sheet, using a spatula.

Gingerbread Cookies

Makes 24 cookies

- 1 package gingerbread mix
- ¼ cup milk
- ¼ cup salad oil
- 2 tablespoons margarine

Preheat oven to 350 degrees F. Pour gingerbread mix into bowl; add milk and salad oil. Mix well. Chill in refrigerator until firm. When chilled, place gingerbread mixture on lightly floured board. Using rolling pin or milk bottle, roll gingerbread over board. It should be about ¼ inch thick. Cut out shapes with round cookie cutter or you can use the top edge of a glass, but wet the rim so that the dough does not stick. Place shapes on greased cookie sheet. Bake in oven 12 minutes.

Coconut Macaroons

Makes 24 cookies

    1 tablespoon butter
2⅔ cups flaked coconut
   ¾ cup sweetened condensed milk
    1 egg, slightly beaten
   ¼ teaspoon vanilla extract
    2 teaspoons margarine

Preheat oven to 325 degrees F. Grease baking sheet with butter. In bowl, combine all ingredients; mix well. Drop mixture by teaspoons onto baking sheet. Bake in oven 20 minutes or until lightly browned. When done, immediately remove from baking sheet with spatula and cool on serving plate.

Chocolate Chip Cookies

Makes 36 cookies

     margarine
    1 package white cake mix
   ½ cup vegetable oil
    2 tablespoons water
    1 egg
    1 package (6 ounces) semisweet
     chocolate pieces

Preheat oven to 350 degrees F. Grease cookie sheet with margarine. Empty cake mix into bowl. Add vegetable oil, water, and egg. Blend until well mixed and smooth. Add chocolate pieces and stir into batter. Drop by teaspoons onto greased cookie sheets about 2 inches apart. Bake in oven 12 to 15 minutes. When done, immediately remove from baking sheet using spatula.

Brownies

Makes 18 bars

1 tablespoon butter or margarine
1 stick of margarine
2 squares (1 ounce each) unsweetened chocolate or 7 tablespoons cocoa
1 cup sugar

½ cup crushed peanuts
½ cup all-purpose flour
1 teaspoon baking powder
2 eggs

Preheat oven to 350 degrees F. .Grease square baking pan with butter. Melt margarine and chocolate squares (or cocoa) in saucepan over low heat. Add sugar, peanuts, flour, and baking powder. Stir to blend. Add eggs and mix well. Pour batter into greased baking pan and bake in oven 30 minutes. When done, remove from oven and place on rack to cool. When cooled, cut into 18 bars.

Multicolored Sprinkle Cookies

Makes 36 cookies

1 tablespoon butter
½ cup melted margarine
1 cup sugar
1 egg
2 tablespoons milk

1 teaspoon lemon juice
1 teaspoon baking soda
2 cups flour
multicolored sprinkles

Preheat oven to 400 degrees F. Grease baking sheets with butter. Pour margarine into bowl. Beat in sugar, egg, milk, and lemon juice until creamy. In second bowl, sift together baking soda and flour; add to creamed mixture. Mix well. Drop mixture by tablespoons 2 inches apart onto baking sheets. Top with a few sprinkles. Bake in oven 8 to 10 minutes or until golden brown. When done, remove from baking sheets at once with spatula and let cool on wire rack.

Shang-Chi's Fortune Cookies

Makes 8 cookies

Fortune cookies are easy to make and fun to serve. You can make up your own personalized messages on small strips of paper and insert one into each fortune cookie. You can make predictions concerning good health and happiness, questions and answers, or any type of message you feel like writing.

¼ cup cake flour
2 tablespoons sugar
1 tablespoon cornstarch
    dash of salt

2 tablespoons cooking oil
1 egg white
1 tablespoon water

In bowl, sift together flour, sugar, cornstarch, and salt. Add oil and egg white; stir until smooth. Add water; mix well. Lightly grease frying pan. Make 1 cookie at a time. Put 1 tablespoon of batter into frying pan, spreading batter to a 3½-inch circle. Cook over low heat for 4 minutes or until lightly browned. Use spatula to turn cookie and cook 1 minute longer. Quickly place cookie on pot holder. Place fortune strip in center. Fold cookie in half and fold again over edge of bowl. Place in muffin pan to cool.

REAL EASY TO BAKE AND DECORATE!

Cutout, or shaped, cookies are easy to make and fun, too. Decide what design you would like the cookie to be. When picking one of your favorite Superheroes, be sure that you can match some of the coloring so that you can identify it. Here are some helpful hints:

• To define small details, use multicolored sprinkles in line form.
• Licorice strips and gumdrops are great for mouths, lines, and eyes.
• Colorful construction paper cut into needed shapes creates an excellent "first appearance," but be sure to remove it before eating.
• Coconut with desired food coloring creates a realistic look.

Cutout Method:

Trace pictures on page 85 (or any other design that you wish) onto a piece of waxed paper. Cut out shape. Place on uncooked dough and trim with pizza cutter or knife. Use pancake turner to place cookie shape on cookie sheet and bake. When done, remove from oven and let cool.

Decorating Method:

Place waxed paper shape on top of cookie (shape may be a little smaller) and use a toothpick to pierce definite outlines for character desired. Fill in with desired colors and decorations to resemble character you want.

For Spider-Man Cookie:

Spread round or oval cookie with strawberry jam and create facial design with black strips of licorice. Crushed marshmallows can be used for eyes.

Basic Cutout Cookie Recipe

    ½ cup margarine
    1 cup sugar
    1 egg
    2 teaspoons baking powder
    2½ cups cake flour
    ½ teaspoon salt
    ½ cup milk
    1 teaspoon vanilla

In large bowl, cream shortening well. Add sugar and egg and blend. Sift baking powder, flour and salt together and add to creamed mixture alternating with the milk. Add vanilla and stir. Cover and chill in refrigerator for 1 hour. Place on floured board. Use rolling pin to roll out dough, making it very thin and flat. Cut out in your shapes. Gently pick up cookie shape (a pancake turner may be helpful) and place on baking sheet. Bake in oven at 350 degrees F 10 to 12 minutes. When done, remove to rack and decorate.

For Captain America Cookie:

White frosting and blueberry jam with red licorice strips.

For Hulk Cookie — All-American Chocolate Style:

Chocolate frosting, black licorice for eyebrows, nose, and mouth; black gumdrops for eyes.

For Thing Cookie:

Spread with lemon pudding; put in freezer for 5 minutes. Decorate with licorice and grape jelly on a knife in zigzag form.

HERE ARE THE SIZES AND SHAPES OF YOUR COOKIES—READ INSTRUCTIONS FOR COLORING!

PLOP!

PiES and

CAPTAIN AMERICA FEATURE

AMERICAN PiE

Makes one 8- or 9-inch pie

Prepared package pie crust
2 cans (1 pound 4 ounces) apples
½ cup brown sugar
½ cup granulated sugar
¼ teaspoon cinnamon
3 teaspoons lemon juice
1 tablespoon margarine

Preheat oven to 425 degrees F. Follow label directions for preparing two-crust pie. In large bowl, combine apples, sugars, cinnamon, and lemon juice. Pour into pastry-lined pie plate; dot with margarine. Place and adjust top crust. Use fork to prick a few openings in top. Bake in oven 40 minutes. When done, remove to a wire rack to cool.

ABOUT PIE CRUSTS

You've got it made with the ready mades! Start with a prepared pie shell and follow the label directions for baking. Graham cracker pie shells need no baking — just fill, chill, and eat. To make quick and easy single-crust pies, select a pudding mix or canned fruit or pie filling, or a combination of both as fillings for the pastry shells. Tart shells are also available in prepared form.

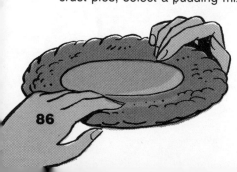

Graham Cracker Pie Crust

Makes one 9-inch pie crust

2 tablespoons margarine
2 cups graham cracker crumbs, finely crushed
¼ cup sugar
2 tablespoons water

In bowl, blend margarine, cracker crumbs, and sugar. Add water and knead mixture gently. Press mixture into bottom and sides of pie pan. Put pan in refrigerator and chill for 1 hour. When chilled, fill with your favorite filling.

SWOOOSH! TARTS

Lemon Coconut Pie

Makes one 8- or 9-inch pie

- 1 (8- or 9-inch) graham cracker pie shell
- 1 package (4½ ounces) mix-and-serve lemon pudding
- 2 cups milk
  prepared whipped cream
- ½ cup shredded coconut

Pour pudding mix into bowl; add milk. Beat slowly with egg beater until blended. Pour pudding into pie shell. Cover with dinner plate or large frying pan cover and chill in refrigerator for 1 hour. Just before serving, top with prepared whipped cream and coconut.

Super Chocolate Pie

Makes one 8-inch pie

- 1½ cups sweetened condensed milk
- 2 squares (1 ounce each) unsweetened chocolate
- ½ cup water
- ½ teaspoon vanilla extract
- 1 baked pastry shell
  prepared whipped cream

Cook milk and chocolate over boiling water until somewhat thickened; stir constantly. Add water gradually; cook about 3 minutes, until mixture thickens further. Add vanilla; pour into pie shell. Let cool ½ hour. Place in refrigerator and let cool for about 3 hours. Before serving, spread on whipped cream.

Ice Cream Pie

Makes one 9-inch pie

- 1 graham cracker pie shell
- 1 quart ice cream, your favorite flavor
  chocolate sprinkles

Fill pie shell with ice cream. Top with whipped cream and sprinkles and serve immediately.

About Tarts

Tart shells are a great base for many different combinations of fillings. Among many are fresh or canned fruits, puddings, ice cream, or cooked vegetables and meats (see pages 49-50).

Try some of the following:
- Crushed pineapple tidbits and a scoop of orange sherbet
- Applesauce and whipped cream and cinnamon
- Fresh blueberries, strawberries, or raspberries topped with a scoop of ice cream.
- Vanilla pudding topped with sliced bananas
- Lemon pudding mixed with raisins
- Make a tart sundae with ice cream and your favorite topping. Add some nuts and cherries for a delicious dessert.

Blueberry Sundae Serves 2

⅓ cup water
3½ tablespoons blueberry-flavored gelatin mix
2 scoops vanilla ice cream
crushed peanuts

Pour water into saucepan and let boil over medium-high heat. Pour gelatin mix into bowl; add water and stir. Put 1 scoop ice cream into each serving dish. Pour hot gelatin over ice cream. Top with peanuts.

Candy Stripe Parfait Serves 4

1 package (3 ounces) cherry, strawberry, or raspberry gelatin
light cream

Prepare gelatin as directed on package, filling parfait glasses to within 2 inches of the rim. Chill until firm, about 3 hours. Pour light cream over top of gelatin. Using a straw, make deep tunnels at intervals around the outside and through the center of the gelatin, allowing the cream to flow into the tunnels. Top with additional cream and fresh fruit.

Banana Split Serves 2

2 ripe bananas
4 scoops ice cream
chocolate syrup
chopped walnuts
whipped cream
maraschino cherries

Peel and cut bananas in halves lengthwise. Arrange 2 halves, canoe fashion, in each serving dish. Place 2 scoops ice cream in center. Pour on syrup; top with whipped cream and walnuts and cherries.

Chocolate Banana Roll-Ups

Serves 4

2 ripe bananas
4 large prepared pancakes
2 cans (8 ounces) chocolate pudding

Turn oven temperature to 350 degrees F. Cut bananas in half lengthwise. Place a banana half on each pancake. Roll pancake and banana, and secure with toothpicks. Grease cookie sheet with margarine. Place Banana Roll-Ups on baking sheet and bake in oven 10 minutes. When done, use tongs to remove to serving plate. Spoon chocolate pudding on top.

Lemon Banana Dessert

Serves 6

1 cup water
¾ cup cold water
1 package (3 ounces) lemon gelatin
1 medium banana, sliced in penny slices
½ cup pineapple tidbits

In saucepan, heat 1 cup water to boiling. Remove from heat; add lemon gelatin, cold water, and lemon juice. Stir until gelatin is dissolved. Chill in refrigerator until thickened, about 2 hours. Then fold in banana slices and pineapple tidbits. Pour into molds; chill until firm. To serve, unmold on lettuce or ice cream.

Mandarin Pudding

Serves 4

1 can (10 ounces) mandarin orange sections
1 package (3 ounces) no-cook vanilla pudding
whipped cream

Drain liquid from canned orange sections into cup. Prepare pudding mix as directed on package, using liquid from orange sections instead of water. Half-fill each serving glass with pudding. Place a few orange sections on top. Fill glasses with remaining pudding. Top with whipped cream.

Coconut Melon Delight

Serves 4

1 package (3 ounces) lime gelatin
1 can (8 ounces) fruit cocktail
2 medium-size melons
coconut

Drain liquid from fruit cocktail into cup. Add ¼ cup water. Prepare gelatin according to directions on package using liquid from fruit cocktail instead of water. Stir in fruit. Let chill in refrigerator at least 3 hours. When ready, cut melons in half. Remove pulp and seeds. Fill each hollow with gelatin. Sprinkle coconut on top.

Chocolate Cream-Filled Doughnuts

Serves 12

12 doughnuts, plain
1 package (3½ ounces) chocolate pudding and pie filling mix
2 cups milk

Prepare pudding with 2 cups milk according to package directions. Cover surface with plastic wrap or dinner plate and refrigerate until cool. Cut each doughnut in half. Spread with pudding and top with other doughnut half.

Cherry Freeze

Makes one 9″ x 5″ x 3″ loaf

1⅓ cups sweetened condensed milk
¼ cup orange juice
1 can (1 pound 5 ounces) cherry pie filling
1 can (9 ounces) crushed pineapple, drained
1 teaspoon vanilla extract
1 pint heavy cream, whipped

In bowl, combine all ingredients, except whipped cream. Mix well. Then gently fold in whipped cream until evenly blended. Pour mixture into loaf pan, 9¼″ x 5″ x 3″. Cover tightly with foil and freeze for 24 hours. When frozen, unmold onto serving tray.

Frozen Pudding Pops

Makes 6 pops

1 package (3 ounces) no-cook pudding mix,
   your favorite flavor

Prepare pudding mix as directed on package. Pour into 5-ounce paper cups. Insert a wooden stick (the type used for ice cream pops) into the center of each cup to use as a handle. Freeze until firm, about 5 hours. When ready, press firmly on bottom of cup to release Pudding Pop.

Popcorn Balls

Makes about 10

2 quarts popped corn
¼ cup sugar
½ cup light corn syrup
½ teaspoon creamy peanut butter
¼ cup cooking oil

Place popcorn in large bowl; set aside. In small saucepan, heat sugar and syrup to boiling, stirring constantly. Remove from heat. Stir in peanut butter. Immediately pour mixture over popcorn, stirring until coated. Grease clean hands with cooking oil and shape popcorn into small balls and place on serving dish.

Apple Dessert

Serves 4

1 can (16 ounces) pie apples
½ cup sugar
½ teaspoon cinnamon
2 tablespoons lemon juice
   miniature marshmallows

Preheat oven to 350 degrees F. Arrange pie apples in baking dish. In bowl, combine sugar, cinnamon, and lemon juice. Sprinkle over apples. Decorate with marshmallows. Bake in oven for 30 minutes.

Peach Melba

Serves 4

1 can (16 ounces) peach halves, drained
1 pint peach ice cream
4 tablespoons raspberry preserves

Place one peach half in each of 4 serving dishes. Place a scoop of ice cream of each peach half. Top with preserves.

Baked Alaska

Serves 8

1 layer of sponge cake about 1 inch thick
1 quart brick ice cream
2 egg whites
1 tablespoon confectioners' sugar
1 teaspoon vanilla

Place cake in baking pan. Top with ice cream, making sure ice cream is about ½ inch from the outer edge of cake. Beat egg whites with sugar until stiff but not dry. Add vanilla. Spread this mixture over ice cream and cake, making sure that the ice cream is covered entirely. Bake in oven set at 450 degrees F for about 8 minutes or until topping is golden brown. Serve at once.

Fruit-Filled Cantaloupe

Serves 4

2 ripe cantaloupes (4 halves)
1 cup blueberries
1 cup seedless grapes
   sugar
   lemon juice
   orange juice

Wash cantaloupes, cut in half, and remove seeds and stringy portion. Fill cavities with blueberries and grapes, using equal portions of each. For each serving, mix 1 teaspoon sugar, ½ teaspoon lemon juice, and 2 tablespoons orange juice. Pour over fruit.

Ice Cream Soda

Serves 2

    4 tablespoons chocolate syrup
    1 bottle (16 ounces) club soda
    2 scoops favorite-flavored ice cream

Put 2 tablespoons of chocolate syrup into each glass. Add ¼ cup club soda to each. Stir to mix. Add 1 scoop of ice cream to each glass and fill with remaining club soda. Stir and serve.

Special Orange Drink

Makes about 7 cups

    1 can (9 ounces) frozen orange juice
       concentrate
    2 cups water
    1 quart ginger ale

Combine concentrate and water, and mix. Add ginger ale and mix well. Pour over ice in tall glasses.

Thick Chocolate Milk Drink

Serves 2

    1½ cups milk
    4 scoops ice cream
    6 tablespoons chocolate-flavored malted milk

Pour milk into bowl. Add 2 scoops of ice cream and beat with egg beater. Add remaining ice cream and malted milk. Beat until foamy. Pour into serving glasses.

Peanut Butter Milk Shake

Serves 2

    1¼ cups milk
    ⅓ cup creamy peanut butter
    1 pint vanilla ice cream

Put milk and peanut butter into container of blender. Blend on high speed until smooth. Add ice cream and blend until it reaches desired thickness.

Purple Cow

Serves 4

    2 cups milk
    1 cup bottled grape soda
    1 pint vanilla ice cream

Combine milk, grape soda, and half of the ice cream in container of blender. Press high speed button and let

mix until thick and foamy. To serve, pour into glasses. Top with remaining ice cream.

Peach Shake

Serves 2

    4 canned peach halves
    6 tablespoons peach syrup
    1 cup cold milk
    3 scoops vanilla ice cream

Put all ingredients into container of blender. Turn blender to medium speed or "Mix" button and blend about 2 minutes. Pour into serving glasses.

Frosty Fruit Punch

Makes 3 quarts

    1½ cups orange juice
    2 cups cranberry juice cocktail
    1 pint raspberry sherbet
    1 bottle (28 ounces) ginger ale, chilled

In large pitcher, pour in orange juice and cranberry juice. Spoon in sherbet. Pour ginger ale over all and stir. Place an ice cube in each glass before serving.

Root Beer Shaker

Serves 2

    1 egg
    3 teaspoons sugar
    ½ teaspoon root beer extract
    4 tablespoons cream
    ¼ cup orange juice
    2 cups milk

Combine all ingredients in container of blender. Blend on medium speed for 2 minutes. Place ice cubes in glasses and serve.

Quick Egg Nog

Serves 4

    2 eggs
    1 quart milk
    1 teaspoon vanilla extract
    ¼ cup sugar
    ¼ teaspoon nutmeg

In bowl, combine all ingredients. Beat with egg beater until creamy, about 3 minutes.

Index